EASY GUITAR

ISBN 0-634-02963-0

Disney characters and artwork © Disney Enterprises, Inc.

Walt Disney Music Company
Wonderland Music Company, Inc.

DISTRIBUTED BY

HAL•LEONARD®
CORPORATION

7777 W. BLUEMOUND RD. P.O. BOX 13819 MILWAUKEE, WI 53213

Visit Hal Leonard Online at
www.halleonard.com

CONTENTS

STRUM AND PICK PATTERNS

This chart contains the suggested strum and pick patterns that are referred to by number at the beginning of each song in this book. The symbols ⊓ and ∨ in the strum patterns refer to down and up strokes, respectively. The letters in the pick patterns indicate which right-hand fingers plays which strings.

p = thumb
i = index finger
m = middle finger
a = ring finger

For example; Pick Pattern 2
is played: thumb - index - middle - ring

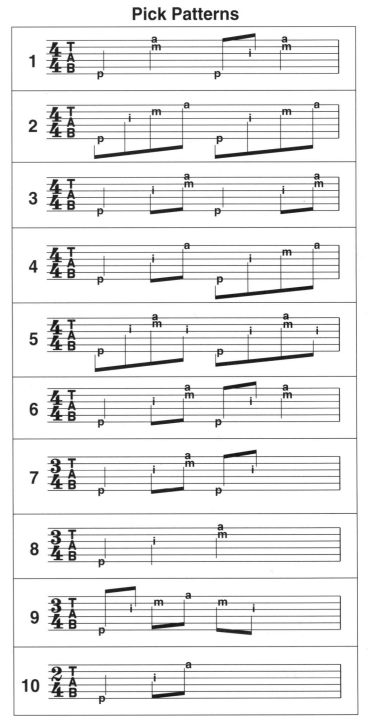

You can use the 3/4 Strum or Pick Patterns in songs written in compound meter (6/8, 9/8, 12/8, etc.). For example, you can accompany a song in 6/8 by playing the 3/4 pattern twice in each measure. The 4/4 Strum and Pick Patterns can be used for songs written in cut time (¢) by doubling the note time values in the patterns. Each pattern would therefore last two measures in cut time.

The Age of Not Believing

from Walt Disney's BEDKNOBS AND BROOMSTICKS

Words and Music by Richard M. Sherman and Robert B. Sherman

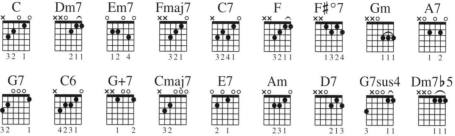

Strum Pattern: 1, 3
Pick Pattern: 2, 6

1. When you rush a - round _____ in hope - less cir - cles _____ search - ing
2., 3. *See Additional Lyrics*

ev - 'ry - where _____ for some - thing true, _____ you're at the age of not be -

liev - ing _____ when all the "Make be - lieve" _____ is through. _____ 2. When you

all, you doubt _____ your - self. You're a cast - a - way _____ where no one

hears you _____ on a bar - ren isle _____ in a lone - ly sea. _____

_____ Where did all the hap - py end - ings go? _____

Where can all the good times be? _____ 3. You must

Coda

there's some-thing won-der-ful, _____ tru-ly won-der-ful _____

_____ in you! _____

Additional Lyrics

2. When you set aside your childhood heroes
And your dreams are lost upon a shelf,
You're at the age of not believing
And worst of all, you doubt yourself.

3. You must face the age of not believing,
Doubting ev'rything you ever knew,
Until at last you start believing
There's something wonderful, truly wonderful in you!

Best of Friends

from Walt Disney's THE FOX AND THE HOUND

Words by Stan Fidel
Music by Richard Johnston

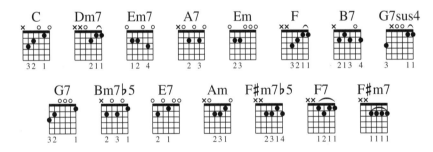

Strum Pattern: 2, 6
Pick Pattern: 4, 6

Verse
Moderately

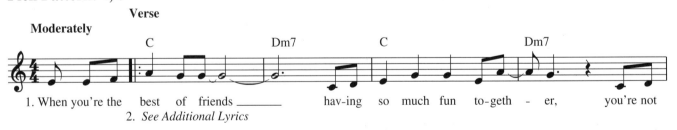

1. When you're the best of friends _____ hav-ing so much fun to-geth-er, you're not
2. *See Additional Lyrics*

e-ven a-ware you're such a fun-ny pair. _ You're the best _ of friends. _ 2. Life's a

Life's one hap - py game.   If on-ly the world would-n't get in the way, —

if on-ly peo-ple would   just let you play.   They'll say you're both be - ing   fools,   you're

break-ing all __ the rules. __   They can't un-der-stand __   your mag - ic

Outro

won - der - land. __   When you're the best of friends, _____   shar-ing

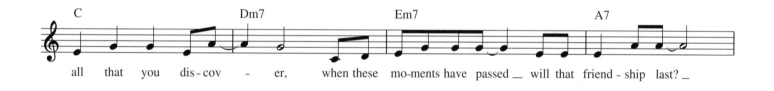

all that you dis-cov - er,   when these mo-ments have passed _ will that friend-ship last? _

Who can say __   if there's a way? _   How I hope, _   I hope it nev - er   ends, _____

__ 'cause you're __ the best of   friends. _____

Additional Lyrics

2. Life's a happy game,
   You could clown around forever.
   Neither of you sees your nat'ral boundaries.
   Life's one happy game.

Alice in Wonderland

from Walt Disney's ALICE IN WONDERLAND

Words by Bob Hilliard
Music by Sammy Fain

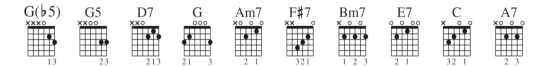

Strum Pattern: 1, 3
Pick Pattern: 2, 4

Moderately

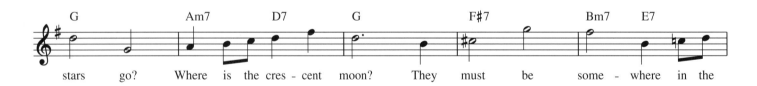

The Ballad of Davy Crockett

from Walt Disney's DAVY CROCKETT

Words by Tom Blackburn
Music by George Bruns

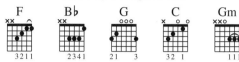

Strum Pattern: 3, 4
Pick Pattern: 3, 4

The Bare Necessities

from Walt Disney's THE JUNGLE BOOK

Words and Music by Terry Gilkyson

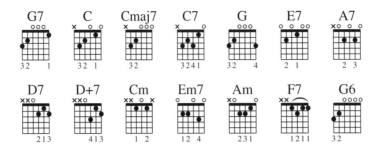

Strum Pattern: 1, 6
Pick Pattern: 2, 4

1. Look for the bare ne - ces - si - ties, __ the sim - ple bare ne -
2., 3. *See Additional Lyrics*

ces - si - ties; __ for - get a - bout your wor - ries and your strife.

I mean the bare ne - ces - si - ties, __ or Moth - er Na - ture's

re - ci - pes __ that bring the bare ne - ces - si - ties __ of life. __

__ Wher - ev - er I wan - der, __ wher - ev - er I roam,

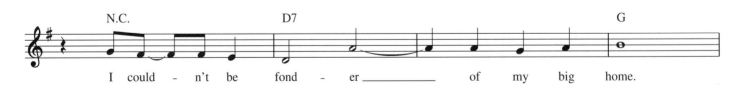

I could - n't be fond - er __ of my big home.

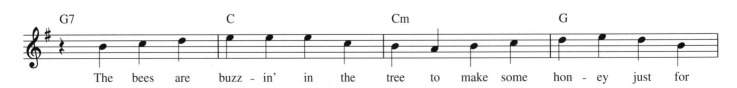

The bees are buzz - in' in the tree to make some hon - ey just for

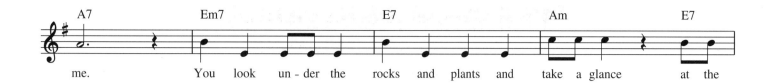

me.   You look un - der the   rocks and plants and   take a glance   at the

fan - cy   ants, __   then   may - be try   a   few.   The bare ne -

ces - si - ties   of   life will come to   you, _____ they'll come to

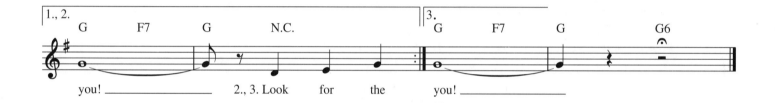

you! _____ 2., 3. Look   for   the   you! _____

Additional Lyrics

2. Look for the bare necessities, the simple bare necessities;
   Forget about your worries and your strife.
   I mean the bare necessities, that's why a bear can rest at ease
   With just the bare necessities of life.
   When you pick a paw-paw or prickly pear,
   And you prick a raw paw next time beware.
   Don't pick the prickly pear by paw,
   When you pick a pear, try to use the claw.
   But you don't need to use the claw
   When you pick a pear of the big paw-paw,
   Have I given you a clue?
   The bare necessities of life will come to you, they'll come to you!

3. Look for the bare necessities, the simple bare necessities;
   Forget about your worries and your strife.
   I mean the bare necessities, or Mother Nature's recipes
   That brings the bare necessities of life.
   So just try to relax (Oh, yeah!) in my back yard,
   If you act like that bee acts you're workin' too hard.
   Don't spend your time just lookin' around
   For something you want that can't be found.
   When you find out you can live without it
   And go along not thinkin' about it.
   I'll tell you something true.
   The bare necessities of life will come to you, they'll come to you!

Beauty and the Beast

from Walt Disney's BEAUTY AND THE BEAST

from Walt Disney's BEAUTY AND THE BEAST: THE BROADWAY MUSICAL

Lyrics by Howard Ashman

Music by Alan Menken

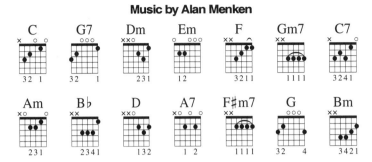

Strum Pattern: 4
Pick Pattern: 2

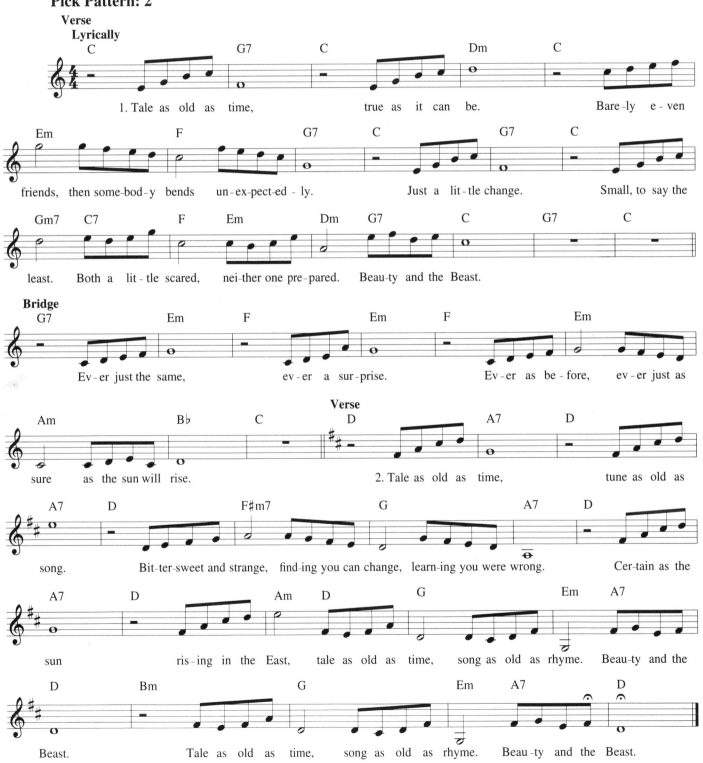

Bella Notte
(This Is the Night)

from Walt Disney's LADY AND THE TRAMP

Words and Music by Peggy Lee and Sonny Burke

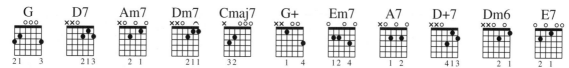

Strum Pattern: 2, 6
Pick Pattern: 3, 5

Slowly

This ___ is the night, ___ it's a beau - ti - ful night, ___ and we call it Bel - la

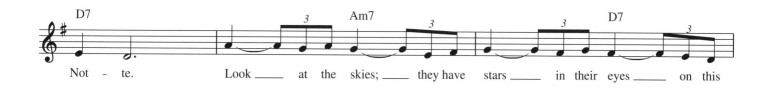

Not - te. Look ___ at the skies; ___ they have stars ___ in their eyes ___ on this

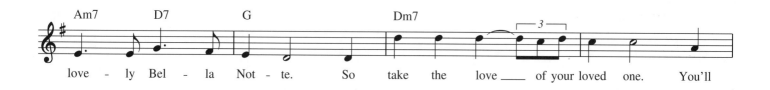

love - ly Bel - la Not - te. So take the love ___ of your loved one. You'll

need it a - bout this time to keep from fall - ing like a star ___ when you

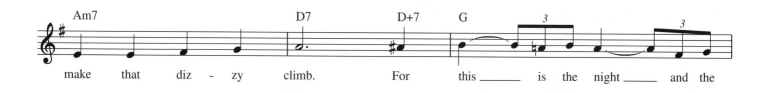

make that diz - zy climb. For this ___ is the night ___ and the

heav - ens are right ___ on this love - ly Bel - la Not - te. ___

Belle

from Walt Disney's BEAUTY AND THE BEAST

Lyrics by Howard Ashman
Music by Alan Menken

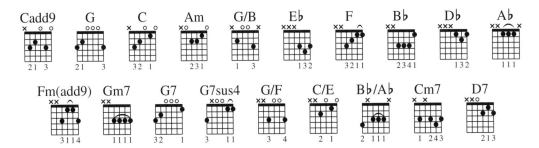

Strum Pattern: 2
Pick Pattern: 3

Verse
 Moderately fast

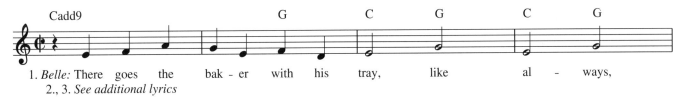

1. *Belle:* There goes the bak - er with his tray, like al - ways,
2., 3. *See additional lyrics*

the same old bread and rolls to sell. Ev-'ry

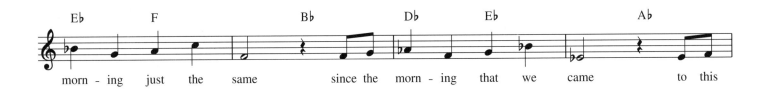

morn - ing just the same since the morn - ing that we came to this

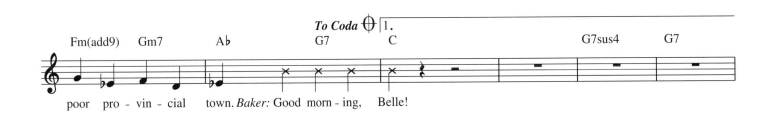

poor pro - vin - cial town. *Baker:* Good morn - ing, Belle!

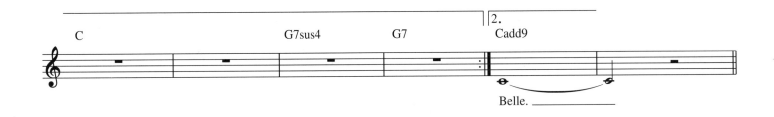

Belle.

Bridge

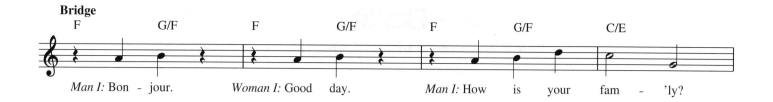

Man I: Bon - jour. Woman I: Good day. Man I: How is your fam - 'ly?

Woman II: Bon - jour. Man II: Good day. Woman II: How is your wife?

Woman III: I need six eggs! Man III: That's too ex - pen - sive. Belle: There

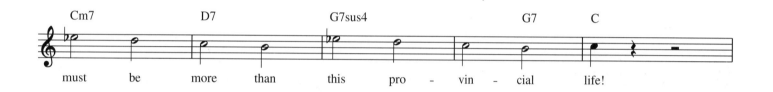

must be more than this pro - vin - cial life!

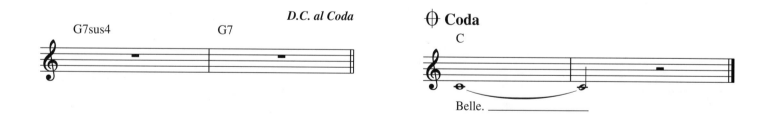

Belle.

Additional Lyrics

2. *Townsfolk:* Look there she goes that girl is strange, no question.
Dazed and distracted, can't you tell?
Never part of any crowd, 'cause her head's up on some cloud.
No denying she's a funny girl, that Belle.

3. *Townsfolk:* Look there she goes that girl is so peculiar.
I wonder if she's feeling well.
With a dreamy far-off look.
And her nose stuck in a book,
What a puzzle to the rest of us is Belle.

Bibbidi-Bobbidi-Boo
(The Magic Song)

from Walt Disney's CINDERELLA
Words by Jerry Livingston
Music by Mack David and Al Hoffman

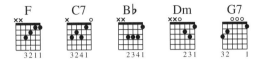

Strum Pattern: 3
Pick Pattern: 3

Brazzle Dazzle Day

from Walt Disney's PETE'S DRAGON

Words and Music by Al Kasha and Joel Hirschhorn

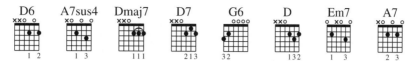

Strum Pattern: 2, 3
Pick Pattern: 3, 4

Verse
Joyfully

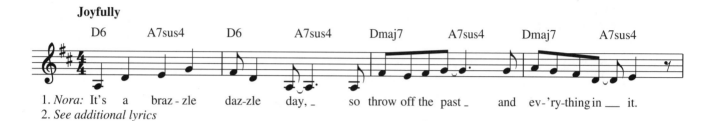

1. *Nora:* It's a braz-zle daz-zle day, __ so throw off the past __ and ev-'ry-thing in __ it.
2. *See additional lyrics*

That's the braz-zle daz-zle way, __ en - joy-ing your time __ from min-ute to min - ute,

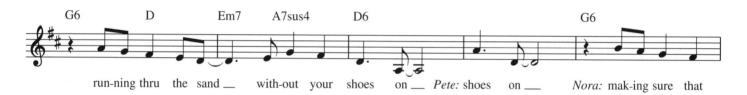

run-ning thru the sand __ with-out your shoes on __ *Pete:* shoes on __ *Nora:* mak-ing sure that

you don't keep your blues on __ braz-zle daz - zle day. _____

2. **Outro**

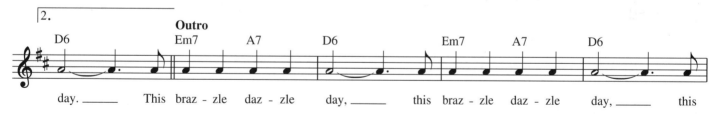

day. _____ This braz-zle daz - zle day, _____ this braz-zle daz - zle day, _____ this

braz-zle daz - zle day, _____ this braz - zle daz - zle day. _____

Additional Lyrics

2. *Nora:* It's a brazzle dazzle day
   When you think of love and never of sorrow.
   To do your work now *Lampie:* and take off tomorrow.
   Flying thru the air you don't need wings on
   Nora & Pete: wings on *Lampie:* climb right up and
   Feel the thrill it brings on a brazzle dazzle day.

Can You Feel the Love Tonight

from Walt Disney Pictures' THE LION KING
Music by Elton John
Lyrics by Tim Rice

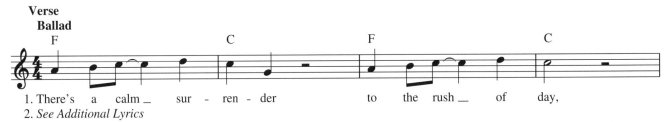

Strum Pattern: 4
Pick Pattern: 4

Verse
Ballad

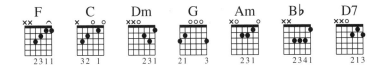

1. There's a calm __ sur - ren - der to the rush __ of day,
2. *See Additional Lyrics*

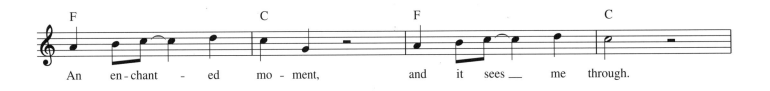

when the heat __ of the roll - ing world __ can be turned __ a - way.

An en - chant - ed mo - ment, and it sees __ me through.

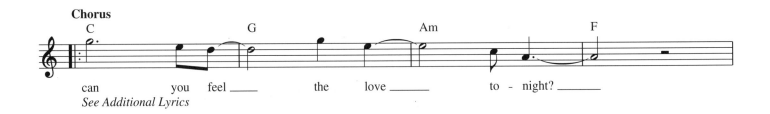

It's e - nough __ for this rest - less war - rior just to be __ with you. And

Chorus

can you feel __ the love __ to - night? _____
See Additional Lyrics

It is where _____ we are? _____

It's e - nough _____ for this wide - eyed _____ wan - der - er

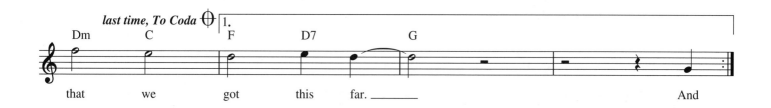

that we got this far. _____ And

ver - y best. _____

ver - y best. _____

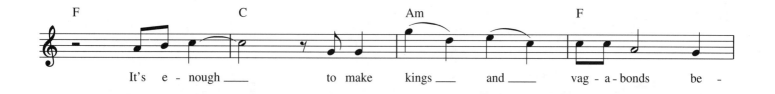

It's e - nough _____ to make kings _____ and _____ vag - a - bonds be -

lieve the ver - y best. _____

Additional Lyrics

2. There's a time for ev'ryone,
   If they only learn
   That the twisting kaleidoscope
   Moves us all in turn.
   There's a rhyme and reason
   To the wild outdoors
   When the heart of this star-crossed voyager
   Beats in time with yours.

Chorus   And can you feel the love tonight,
   How it's laid to rest?
   It's enough to make kings and vagabonds
   Believe the very best.

Candle on the Water

from Walt Disney's PETE'S DRAGON

Words and Music by Al Kasha and Joel Hirschhorn

Strum Pattern: 2
Pick Pattern: 2

Additional Lyrics

2. I'll be your candle on the water,
   'Til ev'ry wave is warm and bright.
   My soul is there beside you,
   Let this candle guide you;
   Soon you'll see a golden stream of light.

3. I'll be your candle on the water,
   This flame inside of me will grow.
   Keep holding on, you'll make it,
   Here's my hand so take it;
   Look for me reaching out to show
   As sure as rivers flow,
   I'll never let you go,

Chim Chim Cher-ee

from Walt Disney's MARY POPPINS

Words and Music by Richard M. Sherman and Robert B. Sherman

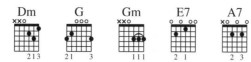

Strum Pattern: 7
Pick Pattern: 8

Additional Lyrics

2. I spends me time in the ashes and smoke,
   In this 'ole wide world there's no 'appier bloke.

Circle of Life

from Walt Disney Pictures' THE LION KING

Disney Presents THE LION KING: THE BROADWAY MUSICAL

Music by Elton John
Lyrics by Tim Rice

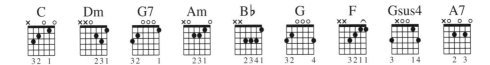

Strum Pattern: 4
Pick Pattern: 2

Cruella De Vil

from Walt Disney's 101 DALMATIANS

Words and Music by Mel Leven

Colors of the Wind

from Walt Disney's POCAHONTAS
Music by Alan Menken
Lyrics by Stephen Schwartz

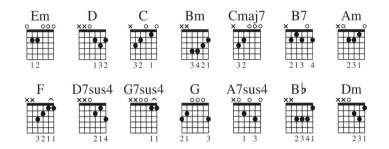

Em D C Bm Cmaj7 B7 Am

F D7sus4 G7sus4 G A7sus4 B♭ Dm

Strum Pattern: 2
Pick Pattern: 2

Intro
Moderately

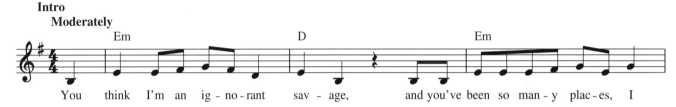

You think I'm an ig-no-rant sav-age, and you've been so man-y plac-es, I

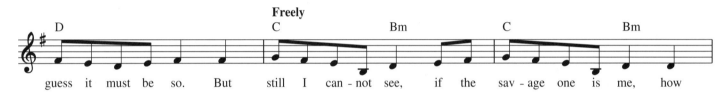

guess it must be so. But still I can-not see, if the sav-age one is me, how

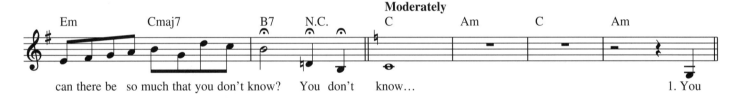

can there be so much that you don't know? You don't know… 1. You

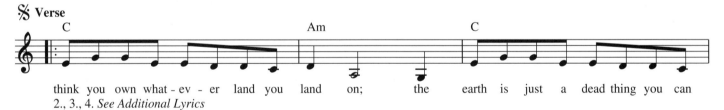

Verse

think you own what-ev-er land you land on; the earth is just a dead thing you can
2., 3., 4. *See Additional Lyrics*

claim; but I know ev-'ry rock and tree and crea-ture has a life, has a spir-it, has a

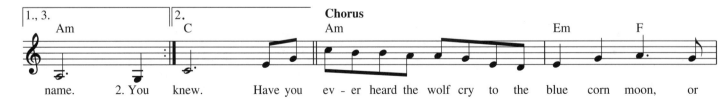

name. 2. You knew. Have you ev-er heard the wolf cry to the blue corn moon, or

asked the grin-ning bob-cat why he grinned? Can you sing with all the voic-es of the

24

D.S. al Coda

Additional Lyrics

2. You think the only people who are people
   Are the people who look and think like you,
   But if you walk the footsteps of a stranger
   You'll learn things you never knew you never knew.

3. Come run the hidden pine trails of the forest,
   Come taste the sunsweet berries of the earth;
   Come roll in all the riches all around you,
   And for once never wonder what they're worth.

4. The rainstorm and the river are my brothers;
   The heron and the otter are my friends;
   And we are all connected to each other
   In a circle, in a hoop that never ends.

A Dream Is a Wish Your Heart Makes

from Walt Disney's CINDERELLA

Words and Music by Mack David, Al Hoffman and Jerry Livingston

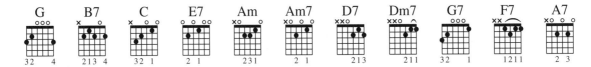

Strum Pattern: 2
Pick Pattern: 4

Ev'rybody Wants to Be a Cat

from Walt Disney's THE ARISTOCATS

Words by Floyd Huddleston
Music by Al Rinker

Strum Pattern: 2
Pick Pattern: 4

Bridge

Come on, scat cat, turn me on, __ I'll take my horn and my best tone, __ then blow a lit-tle soul in-to the

tune.

Let's take it to an-oth-er key, __

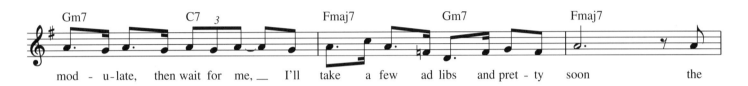

mod - u-late, then wait for me, __ I'll take a few ad libs and pret - ty soon the

oth - er cats will all com-mence __ con - gre-gat - ing on the fence, __ be - neath the al - ley's on - ly light, __ where

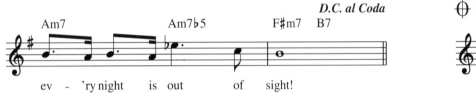

ev - 'ry night is out of sight!

D.C. al Coda

𝄌 *Coda*

be a cat! __

Friend Like Me

from Walt Disney's ALADDIN

Lyrics by Howard Ashman
Music by Alan Menken

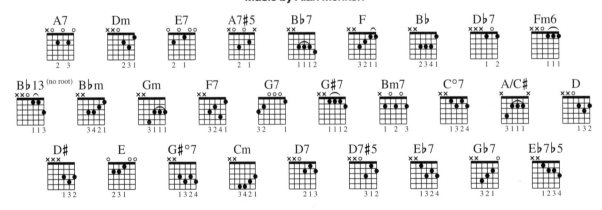

Strum Pattern: 3
Pick Pattern: 3

Verse
Brightly

1. Well, A - li Ba - ba had them for - ty theives. Sche - her - a -

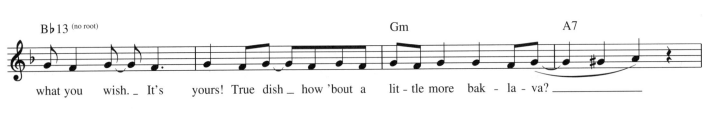

what you wish. _ It's yours! True dish _ how 'bout a lit - tle more bak - la - va? _____

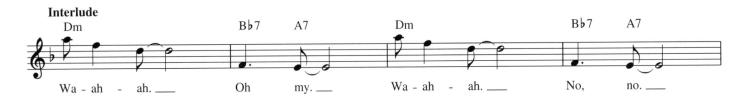

Have some of col - umn "A." _ Try all of col - umn "B." _ I'm

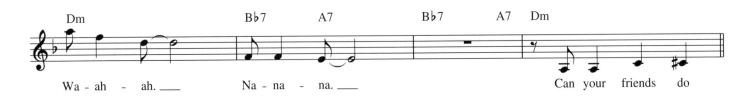

in the mood _ to help you, dude, you ain't nev - er had a friend like me.

Interlude

Wa - ah - ah. _ Oh my. _ Wa - ah - ah. _ No, no. _

Wa - ah - ah. _ Na - na - na. _ Can your friends do

Bridge

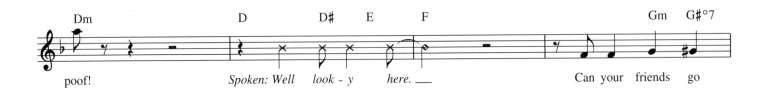

this? Can your friends do that? Can your friends pull

this out their lit - tle hat? _ Can your friends _ go

poof! *Spoken: Well look - y here.* _ Can your friends go

ab - ra - ca - da - bra, let 'er rip and then make the suck - er dis - ap - pear? _ 2. So don-cha

Verse

D7　　　　　Gm　　　　　D7　　　　　Gm

sit there slack-jawed, bug-gy eyed. I'm here to an-swer all your mid-day prayers. _ You got me

D7　　　　　Gm　　　　　A7　　　　　D7♯5

bo - na - fi - de cer - ti - fied. _ You got a ge-nie for your chargé d'af-faires. _ I got a

D7　　　　　Gm　　　　　D7　　　　　Gm

pow-er-ful urge to help you out. So what-cha wish I real-ly want to know. _ You got a

D7　　　　　Gm　　　　　A7　　　　　D7

list that's three miles long _ no doubt. Well, all you got-ta do is rub like so. And oh. _____

Outro

Gm　　　　　E♭7　D7　　　　　Gm　　　　　E♭7　D7

Mis - ter A - lad-din sir, _ have a wish or two or three. _ I'm

B♭　　B♭7　　E♭　　G♭7　　B♭

on the job, _ you big na - bob. You ain't nev-er had a friend, nev-er had a friend, you ain't

G♭7　　　　　E♭7♭5

nev-er had a friend, nev-er had a friend, you ain't nev-er _____ had a _____

D7　　　　　Gm　　Eb　D7　Gm　　　　　E♭7　D7

friend like me. _____ Wa-ah - ah.

Gm　　　　　E♭7　D7　　　　　E♭7　　　　　D7　Gm

Wah-ah - ah. You ain't nev-er had a friend like me. ___ *Ha!*

Feed the Birds

from Walt Disney's MARY POPPINS

Words and Music by Richard M. Sherman and Robert B. Sherman

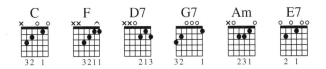

Strum Pattern: 8, 9
Pick Pattern: 8, 9

Feed _____ the birds, tup - pence _____ a bag, tup - pence, _ tup - pence, _

tup - pence _____ a bag. "Feed _____ the birds," that's what _ she cries while o - ver -

head her birds fill the skies. All a - round the ca - the - dral _____ the saints and a - pos - tles _____ look

down as she sells her wares. _____ Al - though you can't see it, _____ you know they are

smil - ing _____ each time some - one shows that he cares. _____ Though _____ her words are

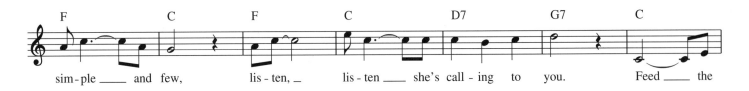

sim - ple _____ and few, lis - ten, _ lis - ten _____ she's call - ing to you. Feed _____ the

birds, tup-pence _____ a bag, tup-pence, _ tup-pence, _ tup - pence a bag.

Following the Leader

from Walt Disney's PETER PAN

Words by Ted Sears and Winston Hibler
Music by Oliver Wallace

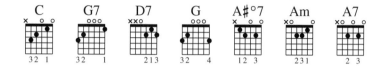

Strum Pattern: 7, 8
Pick Pattern: 7, 8

Verse
Gaily

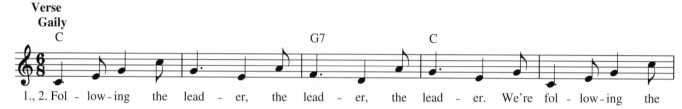

1., 2. Fol - low - ing the lead - er, the lead - er, the lead - er. We're fol - low - ing the

lead - er wher - ev - er he may go. _____ We won't be home till morn - ing, till morn - ing, till

morn - ing. We won't be home till morn - ing be - cause he told us so. Tee

Chorus

dum, tee dee, a tee - dle ee do te day.

{ We're out for
{ We march a -

fun, and this is the game we play. Come on, join in and sing your trou - bles a -
long, and these are the words we say: Tee dum, tee dee, a tee - dle dee - dle dee -

1.

way with a }
ay, oh, a } tee - dle ee dum a tee - dle ee do te day. 2. We're

2.

day. Oh, a tee - dle ee dum a tee - dle ee do te day. _____

Fortuosity

from Walt Disney's THE HAPPIEST MILLIONAIRE

Words and Music by Richard M. Sherman and Robert B. Sherman

Strum Pattern: 3
Pick Pattern: 3

Additional Lyrics

2. Fortuosity, that's me own word.
   Fortuosity, me never feel alone word.
   'Round a corner, under a tree,
   Good fortune's waitin', just wait and see.
   Fortuosity, lucky chances.
   Fortuitious little, happy happenstances.
   I keep smilin' 'cause my philosophy is:
   "Do your best and leave the rest to fortuosity!"

Go the Distance

from Walt Disney Pictures' HERCULES

Music by Alan Menken
Lyrics by David Zippel

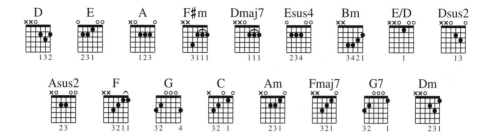

*Strum Pattern: 3
*Pick Pattern: 1

Interlude

Outro

I am on my way. I can go ___ the dis-tance. I don't

care how far, some-how I'll ___ be strong. I know ev-'ry mile will be worth my

while. I would go most an-y-where to find where I be-long.

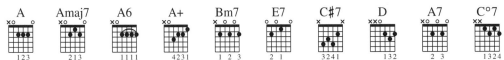

Let's Go Fly a Kite

from Walt Disney's MARY POPPINS

Words and Music by Richard M. Sherman and Robert B. Sherman

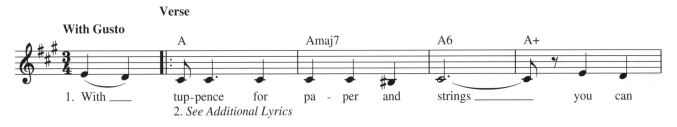

Strum Pattern: 8
Pick Pattern: 8

Verse

With Gusto

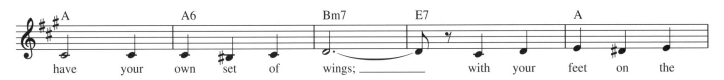

1. With ___ tup-pence for pa - per and strings _____ you can
2. *See Additional Lyrics*

have your own set of wings; _____ with your feet on the

ground you're a bird in flight with your fist hold-ing tight ____

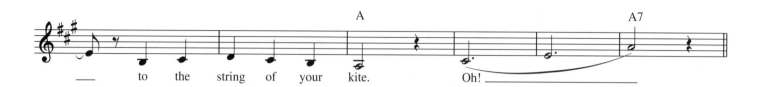
____ to the string of your kite. Oh! ____

Chorus

Let's go fly a kite up to the

high-est height! Let's go fly a kite and

send it soar-ing up through the

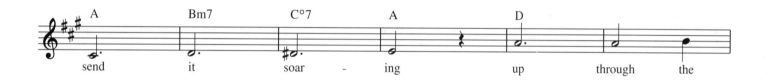
at-mos-phere, up where the air is clear.

Oh, let's go ____ fly a kite! ____

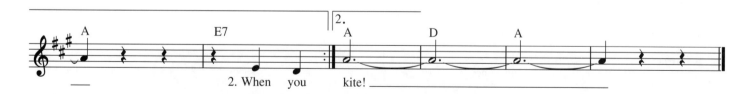
____ 2. When you kite! ____

Additional Lyrics

2. When you send it flying up there,
   All at once you're lighter than air.
   You can dance on the breeze over houses and trees,
   With your fist holding tight to the string of your kite.

God Help the Outcasts

from Walt Disney's THE HUNCHBACK OF NOTRE DAME

Music by Alan Menken
Lyrics by Stephen Schwartz

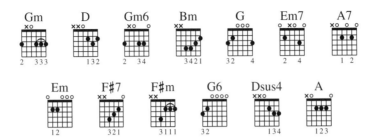

Strum Pattern: 9
Pick Pattern: 7

Verse
Freely

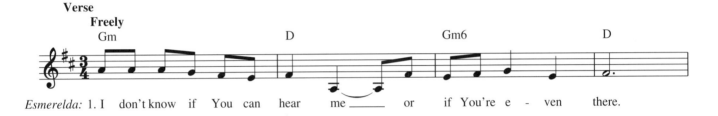

Esmerelda: 1. I don't know if You can hear me _____ or if You're e - ven there.

I don't know if You would lis - ten to a gyp - sy's prayer. Yes, I know I'm just an

out - cast, I should-n't speak to You. Still I see Your face and won - der

Moderately

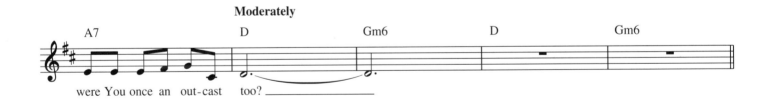

were You once an out-cast too? _____

Chorus

God help _____ the out - casts, hun - gry from birth. Show them _____ the

Hakuna Matata

from Walt Disney Pictures' THE LION KING
Disney Presents THE LION KING: THE BROADWAY MUSICAL

Music by Elton John
Lyrics by Tim Rice

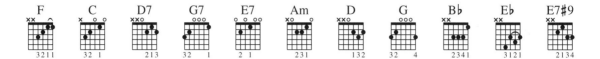

Strum Pattern: 3
Pick Pattern: 4

Chorus

Freely

Timon: Ha - ku - na ma - ta - ta... what a won - der - ful phrase!

Bouncy Shuffle

Pumbaa: Ha - ku - na ma - ta - ta... ain't no pass - ing craze.

Timon: It means no wor - ries ___ for the rest ___ of your days.

Timon & Pumbaa: It's our prob - lem free ___ phi - los - o - phy. ___

Verse

Timon: Ha - ku - na ma - ta - ta. ___ Why, when he was a young wart -

hog... *Spoken:* Very nice. He

Pumbaa: When I was a young wart - hog! *Spoken:* Thanks.

Higitus Figitus

from Walt Disney's THE SWORD IN THE STONE

Words and Music by Richard M. Sherman and Robert B. Sherman

Strum Pattern: 9
Pick Pattern: 7

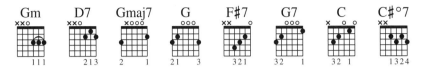

Hig - i - tus fig - i - tus zum - ba - ka - zing, I want your at - ten - tion ev - 'ry-thing! We're pack - ing to leave, come on let's go. Books are al - ways first you know.

Hock - e - ty pock - e - ty wock - e - ty wack, ab - ra - cab - ra dab - ra nack.

Shrink in size ver - y small, we've got to save e - nough room for all.

Hig - i - tus fig - i - tus mig - i - tus mum, pres - ti - dig - i - ton - i - um.

Ci - ce - ro you be - long to the "C's," al - pha - bet - i - cal

or - der please. Al - i - ca - fez bal - a - ca - zez, mal - a - ca - mez mer -

i - pi - des, di - min - ish di - min - ish dic - tion - ar - y that words in your vo -

cab - u - lar - y. Hock - e - ty pock - et - y wock - et - y wack, that's the way __ we

have to pack. Hig - i - tus fig - i - tus mig - i - tus mum, pres - ti - dig - i -

ton - i - um. Hig - i - tus fig - i - tus zoom - a - ca - zam,

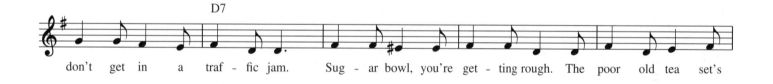

don't get in a traf - fic jam. Sug - ar bowl, you're get - ting rough. The poor old tea set's

cracked e - nough. Hock - et - y pock - et - y wock - et - y wack, odds and ends and

bric a brac. Hig - i - tus fig - i - tus mig - i - tus mum, pres - ti - dig - i -

ton - i - um. Hig - i - tus fig - i - tus mig - i - tus mum, pres - ti - dig - i - ton - i - um.

I Wan'na Be Like You
(The Monkey Song)

from Walt Disney's THE JUNGLE BOOK

Words and Music by Richard M. Sherman and Robert B. Sherman

Strum Pattern: 1, 2
Pick Pattern: 2, 4

Verse
Brightly

1. Now I'm the king of the swing-ers, the jun-gle V. I. P. I've
2., 3. *See Additional Lyrics*

reached the top and had to stop and that's what's both-er-in' me. I wan-na be a man,

man-cub, and stroll right in-to town. And be just like the oth-er men, I'm

Chorus

tired of mon-key-in' 'round! Oh, ooh, ooh, ooh! (Ee - ee.) I wan-na be like you, ooh, ooh! (Ee -

ee.) I wan-na walk like you, talk like you, too, ooh, ooh. (Ee - ee.) You'll see it's

true, ooh, ooh. (Ee - ee.) An ape like me, ee, ee, (Ooh, ooh.) can learn to be

hu - ooh - ooh-man, too, ooh, ooh. (Ee - ee.) 2. Don't too, ooh, ooh. (Ee - ee.)

Additional Lyrics

2. Don't try to kid me, mancub, and don't get in a stew.
   What I desire is man's redfire, so I can be like you.
   Give me the secret, mancub, just clue me what to do.
   Give me the pow'r of man's red flow'r, and make my dream come true!

3. I'll ape your mannerisms, we'll be a set of twins.
   No one will know where mancub ends and orangutan begins.
   And when I eat bananas, I won't peel them with my feet.
   'Cause I'll become a man, mancub, and learn some "Ettikeet."

I'm Late

from Walt Disney's ALICE IN WONDERLAND

Words by Bob Hilliard
Music by Sammy Fain

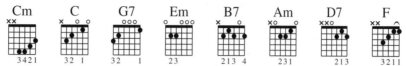

Strum Pattern: 4
Pick Pattern: 1

If I Never Knew You
(Love Theme from POCAHONTAS)

from Walt Disney's POCAHONTAS

Music by Alan Menken
Lyrics by Stephen Schwartz

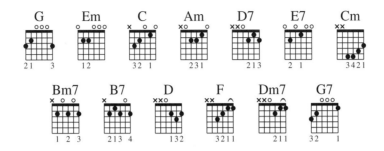

Strum Pattern: 4
Pick Pattern: 4

Intro
Moderately slow

Verse

1. *Male:* If I nev - er knew you,

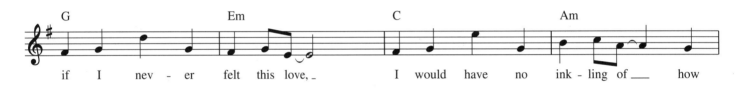

if I nev - er felt this love, _ I would have no ink - ling of ___ how

pre - cious life can be. And if I nev - er held you, I would nev - er

have a clue _ how, at last, _ I'd find in you the miss - ing part of

me. In this world so full of fear, full of rage and lies,

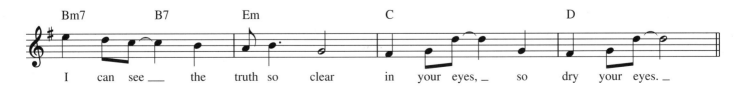

I can see _ the truth so clear in your eyes, _ so dry your eyes. _

Verse

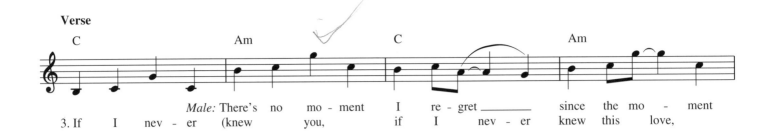

Male: There's no mo - ment I re - gret _____ since the mo - ment
3. If I nev - er (knew you, if I nev - er knew this love,

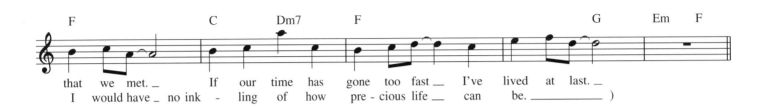

that we met. __ If our time has gone too fast __ I've lived at last. __
I would have __ no ink - ling of how pre - cious life __ can be. _____)

Bridge

Both: I thought our love would be so beau - ti - ful, some - how we'd make the whole

world bright. ___ *Female:* I thought our love would be so beau - ti - ful, we'd turn the dark - ness in -

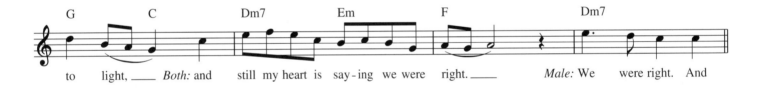

to light, ___ *Both:* and still my heart is say - ing we were right. ___ *Male:* We were right. And

Chorus

if I nev - er (knew __ you, __ I'd have lived my whole life through)
Female: If I nev - er knew you,

emp - ty as ___ the sky, *Both:* nev - er know - ing why,

Freely

lost for - ev - er if I nev - er knew you.
rit.

It's a Small World

from Disneyland and Walt Disney World's IT'S A SMALL WORLD
Words and Music by Richard M. Sherman and Robert B. Sherman

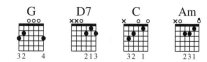

Strum Pattern: 3
Pick Pattern: 3

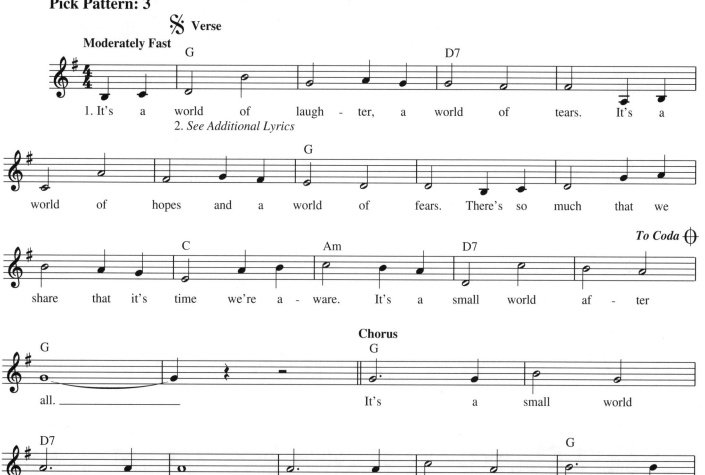

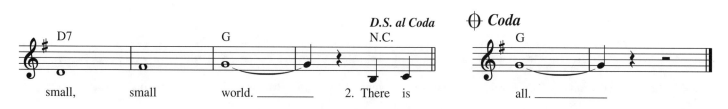

Additional Lyrics

2. There is just one moon and one golden sun,
   And a smile means friendship to ev'ryone.
   Though the mountains divide and the oceans are wide,
   It's a small world after all.

Jolly Holiday

from Walt Disney's MARY POPPINS

Words and Music by Richard M. Sherman and Robert B. Sherman

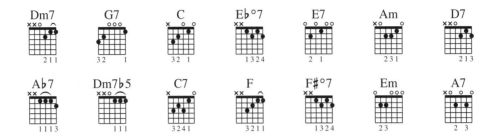

Strum Pattern: 2, 5
Pick Pattern: 1, 4

Lavender Blue
(Dilly Dilly)

from Walt Disney's SO DEAR TO MY HEART

Words by Larry Morey
Music by Eliot Daniel

Strum Pattern: 3, 4
Pick Pattern: 1, 3

Kiss the Girl

from Walt Disney's THE LITTLE MERMAID
Lyrics by Howard Ashman
Music by Alan Menken

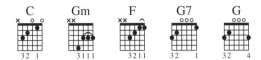

Strum Pattern: 4
Pick Pattern: 3

Verse
Moderately

1. There you see her sitting there across the way.

She don't got a lot to say, but there's something about her. And you

don't know why, but you're dying to try. You wanna kiss the girl.

Yes, you want her. Look at her, you know you do.

Possible she wants you, too. There is one way to ask her. It don't

take a word, not a single word, go on and kiss the girl.

Chorus

Sha, la, la, la, la, la, my oh my. Look like the boy too shy. Ain't gonna kiss the girl.

Verse

2. Now's your mo - ment, _____ float - ing in a blue la - goon. __

Boy, you bet - ter do it soon, _ no time will be bet - ter. _ She don't

say a word _ and she won't _ say a word un - til you kiss the girl.

Chorus

Sha, la, la, la, la, la, don't be scared._ You got the mood pre - pared, _ go on and kiss the girl.

Sha, la, la, la, la, la, don't stop now._ Don't try to hide it how _ you wan - na kiss the girl.

Sha, la, la, la, la, la, float a - long._ And lis - ten to the song, _ the song say kiss the girl.

Sha, la, la, la, la, the mu - sic play. _ Do what the mu - sic say. _ You got - ta kiss the girl.

Outro

You've _ got to kiss the girl. You wan - na kiss the girl.

You've got - ta kiss the girl. Go on and kiss the girl.

Les Poissons

from Walt Disney's THE LITTLE MERM

Lyrics by Howard Ashman
Music by Alan Menken

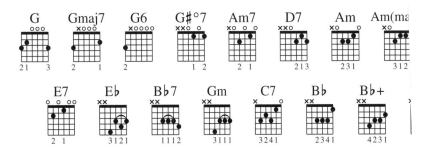

Strum Pattern: 7
Pick Pattern: 7

Verse

Bright Waltz

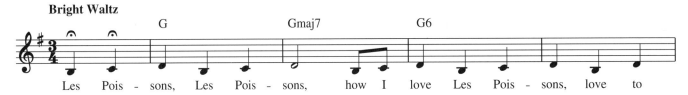

Les Pois - sons, Les Pois - sons, how I love Les Pois - sons, love to

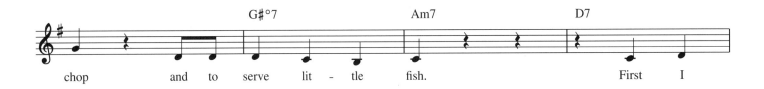

chop and to serve lit - tle fish. First I

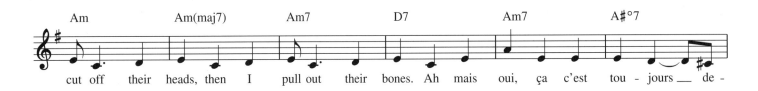

cut off their heads, then I pull out their bones. Ah mais oui, ça c'est tou - jours __ de -

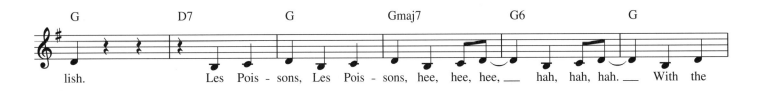

lish. Les Pois - sons, Les Pois - sons, hee, hee, hee, __ hah, hah, hah. __ With the

cleav - er I hack them in two. I pull out what's in - side and I

serve it up fried. God, I love lit - tle fish - es, don't you? _____ Here's

Bridge

some - thing for tempt - ing the pal - ate, _____ pre -

pared in the clas - sic tech - nique. First you pound the fish flat with a

mal - let. _____ Then you slash through the skin, give the bel - ly a

slice, then you rub some salt in 'cause that makes it taste nice. Sa - cre

Outro

bleu! What is this? How on earth could I miss such a

sweet lit - tle suc - cu - lent crab? Quel dom - mage. What a

loss. Here we go in the sauce. Now some flour ___ I think, just a

dab. Now I stuff you with bread. It don't hurt 'cause you're dead. And you're

cer - tain - ly luck - y you are. 'Cause it's gon - na be hot in my

big sil - ver pot. Too - dle loo, mon pois - sons, au re - voir!

Let's Get Together

from Walt Disney Pictures' THE PARENT TRAP

Words and Music by Richard M. Sherman and Robert B. Sherman

Strum Pattern: 2
Pick Pattern: 4

Additional Lyrics

2. Let's get together. Yeah, yeah, yeah!
Think of all that we could share.
Let's get together.
Ev'ry day, ev'ry way and ev'rywhere.
And though we haven't got a lot,
We could be sharin' all we got together.

Little April Shower

from Walt Disney's BAMBI

Words by Larry Morey
Music by Frank Churchill

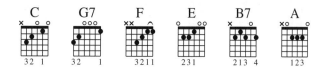

Strum Pattern: 1, 3
Pick Pattern: 2, 6

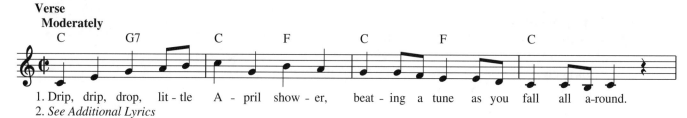

1. Drip, drip, drop, lit-tle A-pril show-er, beat-ing a tune as you fall all a-round.
2. *See Additional Lyrics*

To Coda

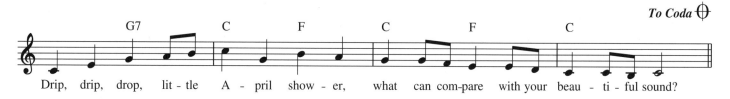

Drip, drip, drop, lit-tle A-pril show-er, what can com-pare with your beau-ti-ful sound?

Bridge

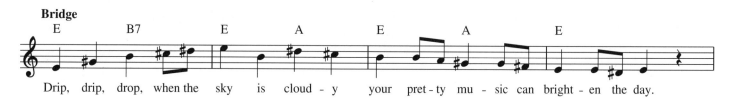

Drip, drip, drop, when the sky is cloud-y your pret-ty mu-sic can bright-en the day.

D.C. al Coda

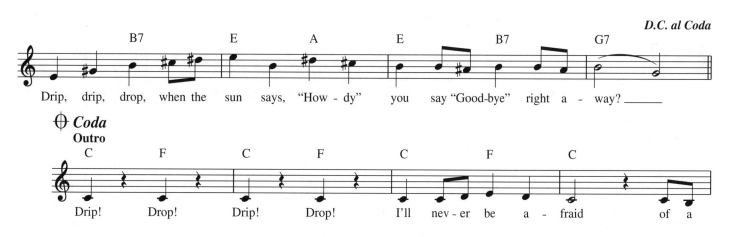

Drip, drip, drop, when the sun says, "How-dy" you say "Good-bye" right a-way? _____

Coda
Outro

Drip! Drop! Drip! Drop! I'll nev-er be a-fraid of a

good lit-tle gay lit-tle A-pril ser-e-nade. _____

Additional Lyrics

2. Drip, drip, drop, little April shower,
   Beating a tune ev'rywhere that you fall.
   Drip, drip, drop, little April shower,
   I'm getting wet and I don't care at all.

Mickey Mouse March

from Walt Disney's THE MICKEY MOUSE CLUB

Words and Music by Jimmie Dodd

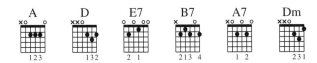

*Strum Pattern: 10
*Pick Pattern: 10

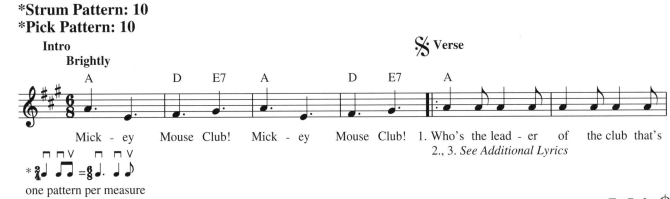

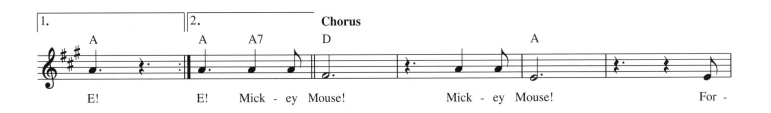

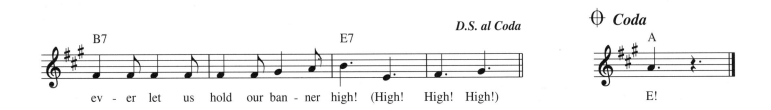

Additional Lyrics

2. Hey, there, Hi, there! Ho, there!
   You're as welcome as can be!
   M-I-C-K-E-Y M-O-U-S-E!

3. Come along and sing a song
   And join the jamboree!
   M-I-C-K-E-Y M-O-U-S-E!

My Funny Friend and Me

from Walt Disney Pictures' THE EMPEROR'S NEW GROOVE

Music by Sting and David Hartley
Lyrics by Sting

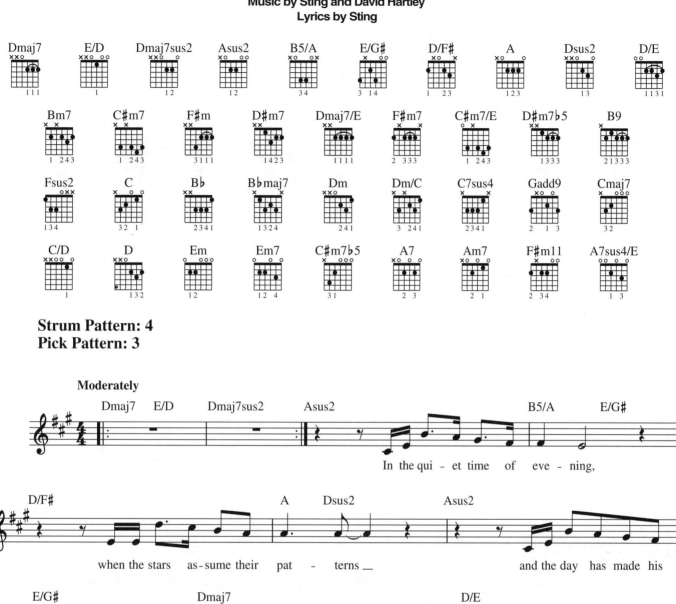

Strum Pattern: 4
Pick Pattern: 3

Moderately

In the qui - et time of eve - ning,

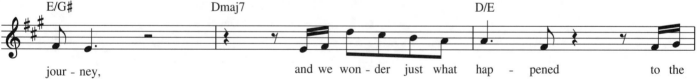

when the stars as-sume their pat - terns _____ and the day has made his

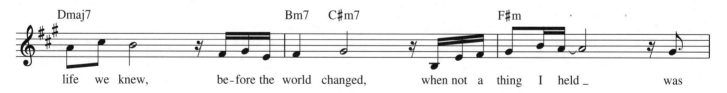

jour - ney, and we won - der just what hap - pened to the

life we knew, be-fore the world changed, when not a thing I held _____ was

true. But you were kind to me, and you re-mind - ed me _____

that the world is not my play - ground; _____ there are oth - er things that

mat - ter; ___ what is sim - ple needs pro - tect - ing.

My il - lu - sions all would shat - ter, ___ but you stayed ___ in my

cor - ner. ___ The on - ly world I knew_ was up - side ___ down,

and now the world and me will know you car - ried me. _ You see the pat - terns in the

big sky; ___ those con - stel - la - tions look like you and I. ___

Just like the pat - terns in the big sky, ___ we could be lost; we could re -

fuse to try. But to have made it through _ in the dark night, ___

who would those luck - y guys _ turn out to be, but that un - us - ual blend _

of my fun - ny friend_ and me. I'm not as clev - er as I thought

I was. ___ I'm not the boy I used to be, be - cause ___

you showed me some - thing dif - f'rent; you showed ___ me some - thing pure. ___

Never Smile at a Crocodile

from Walt Disney's PETER PAN

Words by Jack Lawrence
Music by Frank Churchill

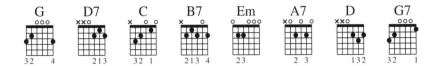

Strum Pattern: 3, 5
Pick Pattern: 3, 4

Verse
Moderately Slow

Nev - er smile at a croc - o - dile, no, you can't get friend - ly with a

croc - o - dile. Don't be tak - en in by his wel - come grin, he's im -

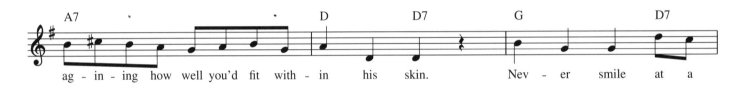

ag - in - ing how well you'd fit with - in his skin. Nev - er smile at a

croc - o - dile, nev - er tip your hat and stop to talk a while. { Nev - er run, walk a - way, say "Good-
{ Don't be rude, nev - er mock, throw a

Fine

night" not "Good-day!" } Clear the aisle and nev - er smile at Mis - ter Croc - o - dile.
kiss, not a rock. }

Bridge

You may ver - y well be well - bred, lots of et - ti - quette in your head,

D.C. al Fine

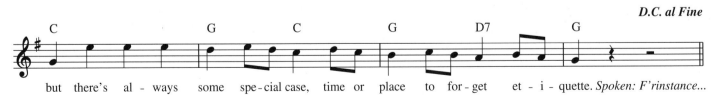

but there's al - ways some spe - cial case, time or place to for - get et - i - quette. *Spoken: F'rinstance...*

Old Yeller

from Walt Disney's OLD YELLER

Words by Gil George
Music by Oliver Wallace

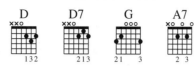

D   D7   G   A7

Strum Pattern: 3, 4
Pick Pattern: 1, 3

Verse
Moderately bright

1. Old Yel - ler was a mon - grel, an ug - ly, lop - eared mon - grel;
2., 3., 4. *See additional lyrics*

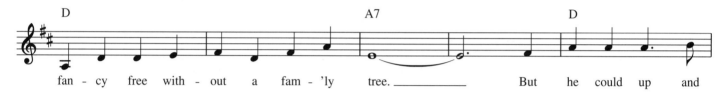

fan - cy free with - out a fam - 'ly tree. _____ But he could up and

do it and prove there's noth - ing to it, and that's how a good dog should

Chorus

be! _____ Here Yel - ler, _____ come back, Yel - ler! _____

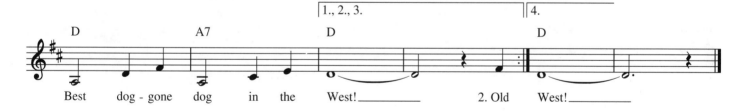

|1., 2., 3. ||4.

Best dog - gone dog in the West! _____ 2. Old West! _____

Additional Lyrics

2. Old Yeller was a hunter,
   A rarin' tearin' hunter;
   In any chase he knew just how to run.
   And when he hunted trouble
   He always found it double,
   And that's when Old Yeller had fun!

3. Old Yeller was a fighter,
   A rootin' tootin' fighter.
   In any scrap he knew just what to do.
   A rough and ready fellow,
   Although his coat was yellow,
   His bold Texas heart was true blue.

4. Young Yeller's just a puppy,
   A little, lop-eared puppy.
   It's plain to see he has a fam'ly tree.
   The image of his pappy,
   He's frisky and he's happy,
   And that's how a good pup should be.

Once Upon a Dream

from Walt Disney's SLEEPING BEAUTY

Words and Music by Sammy Fain and Jack Lawrence
Adapted from a Theme by Tchaikovsky

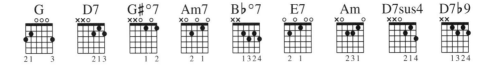

Strum Pattern: 7, 8
Pick Pattern: 7, 8

Moderately Slow

I know you! I walked with you once up - on a

dream. I know you! The gleam in your

eyes is so fa - mil - iar a gleam. Yet, I know it's

true that vi - sions are sel - dom all they seem, but if

I know you, I know what you'll do: you'll love me at one the

way you did once up - on a dream.

Rumbly in My Tumbly

from Walt Disney's THE MANY ADVENTURES OF WINNIE THE POOH

Words and Music by Richard M. Sherman and Robert B. Sherman

Strum Pattern: 6
Pick Pattern: 4

Verse

Moderate Latin

1. Hum - dum de dum hum - de - dum dum, I'm so rum - bly in my tum - bly.
2. *See additional lyrics*

Time to munch an ear - ly lun - cheon, time for some - thing sweet! Oh, I would - n't climb this

tree if a pooh flew like a bee. But I would - n't be a

bear then, so I guess I would - n't care then! Bears love hon - ey and I'm a pooh bear,

so I do care, so I'll climb there. I'm so rum - bly in my tum - bly,

1. time for some - thing sweet!

2. sweet to eat!

Additional Lyrics

2. I don't need a pot of honey.
   I'd be grateful for a platefull.
   When I'm rumbly in my tumbly,
   Then it's time to eat!
   It's the tasteful thing to do,
   Be it ten or twelve or two.
   For anytime is food time,
   When you set your clock on pooh time!

Part of Your World

from Walt Disney's THE LITTLE MERMAID

Lyrics by Howard Ashman
Music by Alan Menken

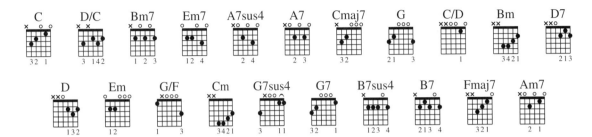

Strum Pattern: 2
Pick Pattern: 3

Verse

Moderately

Look at this stuff. _ Is-n't it neat? _ Would-n't you think _ my col - lec-tion's com-plete?

Would-n't you think _ I'm the girl, ___ the girl who has ev - 'ry - thing. _

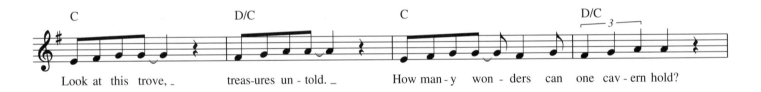

Look at this trove, _ treas-ures un - told. _ How man - y won - ders can one cav - ern hold?

Look-ing a - round _ here you'd think, __ sure, she's got ev - 'ry - thing. _ I've got

Pre-Chorus

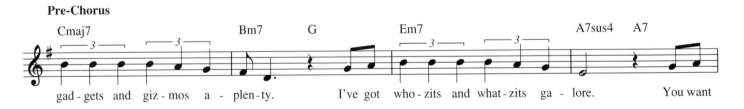

gad - gets and giz - mos a - plen-ty. I've got who - zits and what - zits ga - lore. You want

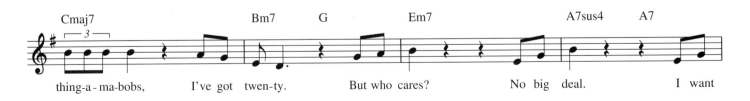

thing-a-ma-bobs, I've got twen-ty. But who cares? No big deal. I want

67

What's a fire, ___ and why does it, what's the word, burn? When's it my turn? Would-n't I

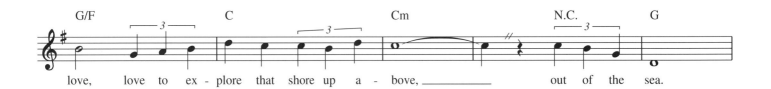

love, love to ex - plore that shore up a - bove, ___ out of the sea.

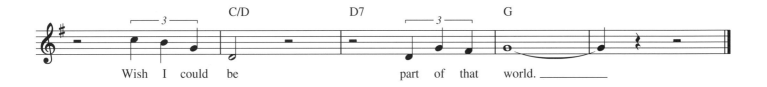

Wish I could be part of that world. ___

Someday

from Walt Disney's THE HUNCHBACK OF NOTRE DAME

Music by Alan Menken
Lyrics by Stephen Schwartz

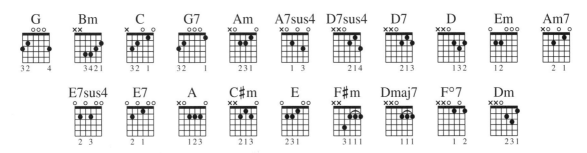

Strum Pattern: 9
Pick Pattern: 9

Verse

Gently

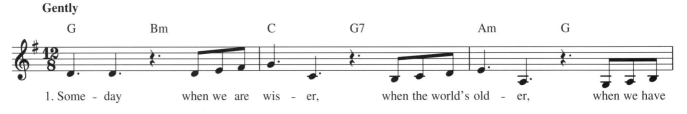

1. Some - day when we are wis - er, when the world's old - er, when we have

learned. I pray some - day we may yet live to

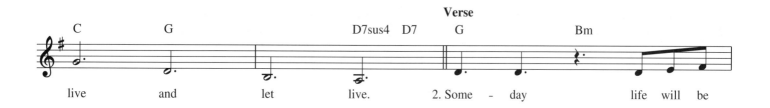

live and let live. 2. Some - day life will be

fair - er, need will be rar - er, greed will not pay. God - speed this bright mil -

len - ni - um on its way. Let it come some - day.

Interlude

Verse

3. Some - day our fight will be won then, we'll stand in the sun then, that bright af - ter -

noon. Till then, on days when the sun is gone,

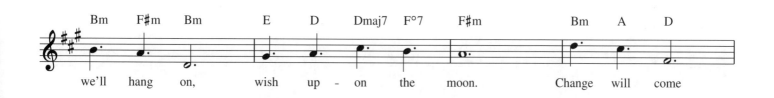

we'll hang on, wish up - on the moon. Change will come

Outro

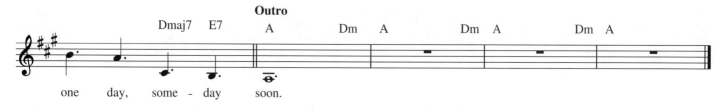

one day, some - day soon.

Perfect Isn't Easy

from Walt Disney's OLIVER & COMPANY

Words by Jack Feldman and Bruce Sussman
Music by Barry Manilow

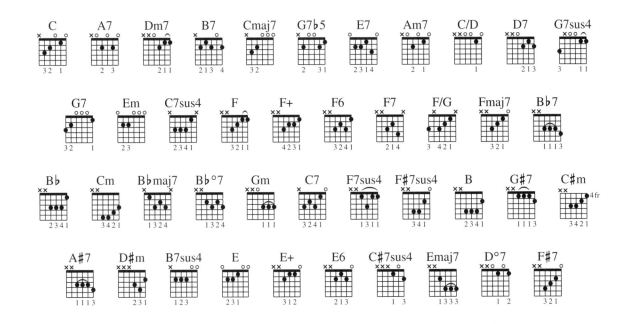

Strum Pattern: 2
Pick Pattern: 4

world says "Yes,"_ then who am I to say "No." Don't ask a mutt to strut _ like a show-girl;

no, girl, you need a "Pro." Not a flea or a flaw.

Take a peek at that paw. La, _____ la, la, la. Per - fec-tion be - comes me *n'est ce pas?*

Un - riv - aled, un - ruf - fled, I'm beau-ty un-leashed, yeah! Jarred rock,

hard sock. So clas-sic and clas-sy, we're not talk-ing Las-sie and ah! _____

_____ Ah! Ooh. _____ *Barking sounds: "Woof, woof, woof."* _

_____ Though man - y cov-et my bone and bowl, _ they're bark-ing up _ the wrong

tree. You pret - ty pups all o - ver the cit - y, I have your heart and you _ have my pit - y.

Pret - ty is nice but still ___ it's just pret-ty. Per-fect, my dears, _____ is me. _____

Uh!

Reflection

from Walt Disney Pictures' MULAN

Music by Matthew Wilder
Lyrics by David Zippel

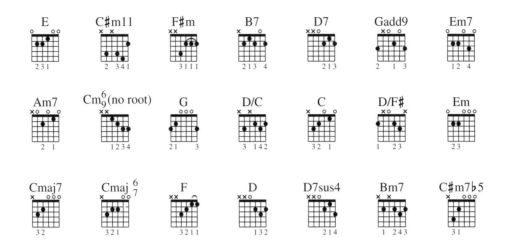

Strum Pattern: 2
Pick Pattern: 4

Verse

Moderately slow

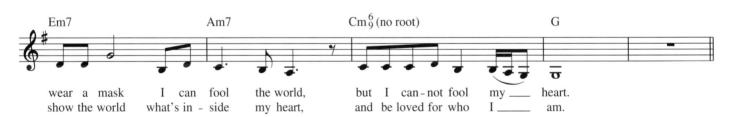

1. Look at me, you may think you see who I real-ly am, but you'll nev-er know me.

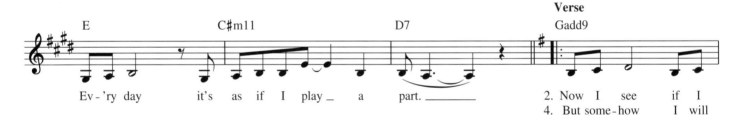

Ev-'ry day it's as if I play a part.

2. Now I see if I
4. But some-how I will

wear a mask I can fool the world, but I can-not fool my heart.
show the world what's in-side my heart, and be loved for who I am.

Chorus

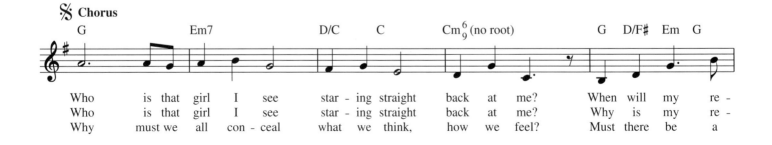

Who is that girl I see star-ing straight back at me? When will my re-
Who is that girl I see star-ing straight back at me? Why is my re-
Why must we all con-ceal what we think, how we feel? Must there be a

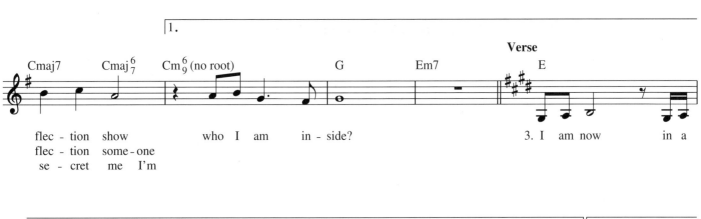

flec - tion show who I am in - side?
flec - tion some - one
se - cret me I'm

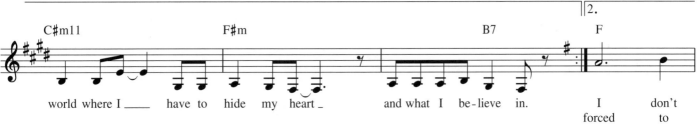

world where I ____ have to hide my heart ____ and what I be - lieve in. I don't
forced to

know? Must I pre - tend that I'm some - one else for all time?
hide? I won't pre - tend that I'm some - one else for all time.

To Coda ⊕   **Pre-Chorus**

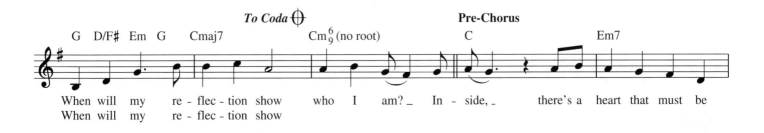

When will my re - flec - tion show who I am? ___ In - side, ___ there's a heart that must be
When will my re - flec - tion show

D.S. al Coda
(take 2nd ending)

free to fly, ___ that burns with a need to know the rea - son ___ why. ___

⊕ **Coda**

who I am in - side? _____ When will my ___ re - flec - tion show

who I am ___ in - side? _____

The Second Star to the Right

from Walt Disney's PETER PAN

Words by Sammy Cahn
Music by Sammy Fain

Strum Pattern: 3
Pick Pattern: 4

The Siamese Cat Song

from Walt Disney's LADY AND THE TRAMP

Words and Music by Peggy Lee and Sonny Burke

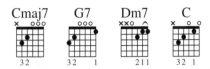

Strum Pattern: 1, 2
Pick Pattern: 2, 4

Slowly

We are Si - am - ee - iz if you plee - iz. We are Si - am - ee - iz if you

don't please. We are for - mer res - i - dents of Si - am.

There {is/are} no fin - er cats than {I/we} am.

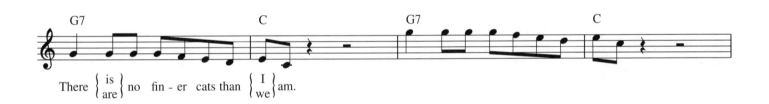

We are Si - am - ese with ver - y dain - ty claws. Please ob - serv - ing paws con - tain - ing

dain - ty claws. Now we look - in' o - ver our new dom - i - cile.

If we like we stay for may - be quite a-while.

So This Is Love
(The Cinderella Waltz)

from Walt Disney's CINDERELLA

Words and Music by Mack David, Al Hoffman and Jerry Livingston

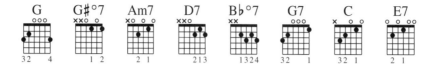

Strum Pattern: 7, 8
Pick Pattern: 7, 8

Tenderly

So this is love, mm, _____ so this is love. _____ So this is what

makes life _____ di - vine. _____ I'm all a - glow, mm, _____ and now I know _____

_____ the key to all heav - en _____ is mine. _____ My heart has

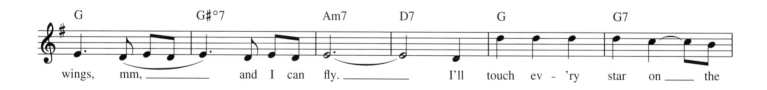

wings, mm, _____ and I can fly. _____ I'll touch ev - 'ry star on _____ the

sky. _____ So this is the mir - a - cle _____ that I've been dream - ing

of, mm, _____ mm, _____ so this is love. _____

A Spoonful of Sugar

from Walt Disney's MARY POPPINS
Words and Music by Richard M. Sherman and Robert B. Sherman

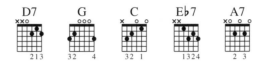

Strum Pattern: 4
Pick Pattern: 5

1. In ev - 'ry job that must be done there is an el - e - ment of
2. *See Additional Lyrics*

fun. You find the fun and snap the job's a game. ____

____ And ev - 'ry task you un - der - take be - comes a piece of

cake, a lark! A spree! It's ver - y clear to

see that a spoon - ful of su - gar helps the med - i - cine go

down, the med - i - cine go down, ____ med - i - cine go down. Just a

spoon - ful of sug - ar helps the med - i - cine go down in a most de -

spoon - ful of sug - ar helps the med - i - cine go down in a most de -

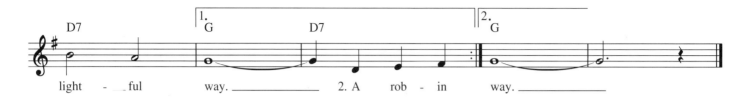

light - ful way. _____ 2. A rob - in way. _____

Additional Lyrics

2. A robin feathering his nest has very little time to rest
   While gathering his bits of twine and twig.
   Though quite intent in his pursuit he has a merry tune to toot.
   He knows a song will move the job along.
   For a...

Strangers Like Me

from Walt Disney Pictures' TARZAN ™

Words and Music by Phil Collins

Strum Pattern: 2
Pick Pattern: 4

Intro

Moderately fast

A D/A A G/A A D/A A G/A

Verse

A D/A A G/A A D/A

1. What - ev - er you do   I'll do it too.   Show me ev - 'ry - thing and
2. *See additional lyrics*

A G/A A D/A A G/A

tell me __ how. __   It all __ means some - thing   and yet noth - ing __ to

Pre-Chorus

A D/A A G/A D G

me.   Oh, I can see there's so much __ to learn; __ it's
See additional lyrics

all so close _ and yet _ so far. _   I see my-self as peo - ple see me. Oh,

𝄋 Chorus

I just know_ there's some - thing big - ger out there. I wan-na know. Can you show _ me?

I wan-na know 'bout these stran - gers _ like _ me. Tell me more; _ please show _ me.

To Coda ⊕ **Bridge**

Some-thing's fa - mil-iar 'bout these stran - gers _ like _ me. Come with me now to see my

world where there's beau - ty be - yond your dreams. Can you feel the things _ I

feel right now with you? _ Take my

hand; there's a world I need to know. _

D.S. al Coda   ⊕ **Coda**

I wan - na know.

Additional Lyrics

2. Ev'ry gesture, ev'ry move that she makes
Makes me feel like never before.
Why do I have this growing need
To be beside her?

Pre-Chorus   Oh, these emotions I never knew,
Of some other world far beyond this place.
Beyond the trees, above the clouds.
Oh, I see before me a new horizon.

Something There

from Walt Disney's BEAUTY AND THE BEAST

Lyrics by Howard Ashman
Music by Alan Menken

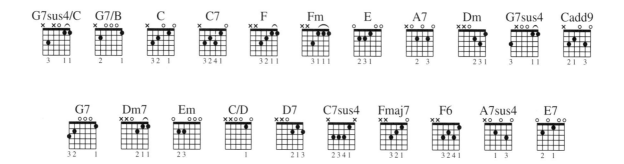

Strum Pattern: 3
Pick Pattern: 2

Verse

Slowly

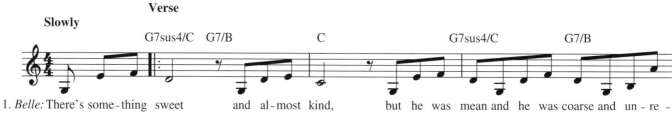

1. *Belle:* There's some-thing sweet and al-most kind, but he was mean and he was coarse and un-re-
2. *See additional lyrics*

fined. And now he's dear, and so I'm sure I won-der why I did-n't see it there _ be-

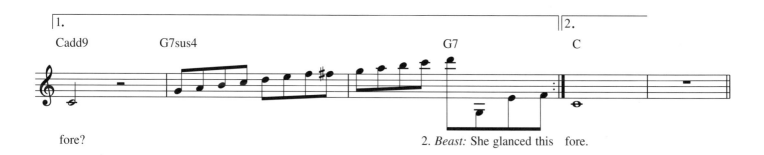

fore?

2. *Beast:* She glanced this fore.

Bridge

Belle: New, _____ and a bit a-larm-ing. Who'd have ev-er thought that

this   could   be? _____   True _____   that he's no   Prince

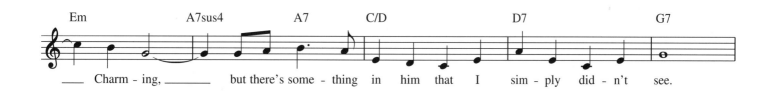

__ Charm - ing, _____   but there's some - thing in   him   that   I   sim - ply   did - n't   see.

Outro-Verse

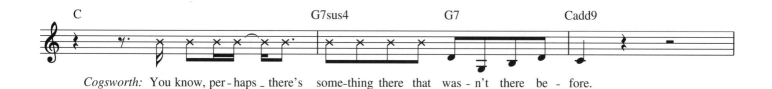

Lumiere: Well, who'd have thought?   *Cogsworth:* Well, who'd have known?   *Lumiere:*   And who'd have
Mrs. Potts: (Well, bless my soul.   Well, who in - deed?

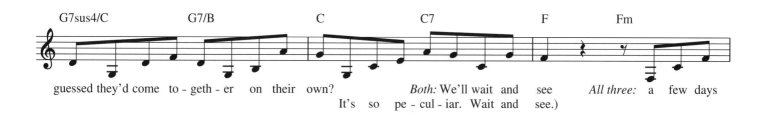

guessed they'd come to - geth - er   on their own?   *Both:* We'll wait and   see   *All three:* a   few days
It's   so   pe - cul - iar. Wait and   see.)

more.   There   may   be   some - thing there   that   was - n't   there   be - fore.

Cogsworth: You know, per - haps _ there's   some - thing there   that   was - n't   there   be - fore.

Mrs. Potts: There   may   be   some - thing   there   that   was - n't   there   be - fore.

Additional Lyrics

2. *Beast:* She glanced this way, I thought I saw,
     And when we touched she didn't shudder at my paw.
     No, it can't be. I'll just ignore.
     But then she's never looked at me that way before.

Stay Awake

from Walt Disney's MARY POPPINS

Words and Music by Richard M. Sherman and Robert B. Sherman

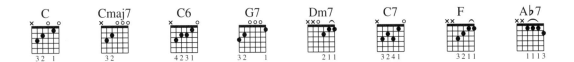

Strum Pattern: 6
Pick Pattern: 2

Verse
Slowly

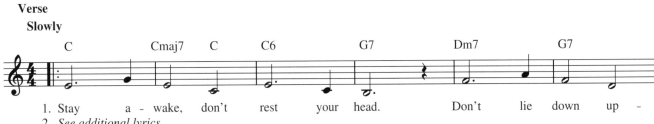

1. Stay a - wake, don't rest your head. Don't lie down up -
2. *See additional lyrics*

on your bed. While the moon drifts in the skies,

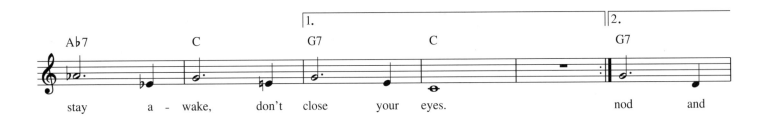

stay a - wake, don't close your eyes. nod and

dream. Stay a - wake, don't nod and dream. _____

Additional Lyrics

2. Though the world is fast asleep,
Though your pillow's soft and deep,
You're not sleepy as you seem.
Stay awake, don't nod and dream.
Stay awake, don't nod and dream.

Supercalifragilisticexpialidocious

from Walt Disney's MARY POPPINS

Words and Music by Richard M. Sherman and Robert B. Sherman

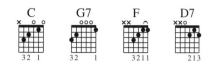

Strum Pattern: 4
Pick Pattern: 3

Chorus
Fast

Sup - er - cal - i - frag - il - is - tic - ex - pi - al - i - do - cious!

E - ven though the sound of it is some - thing quite a - tro - cious.

If you say it loud e - nough you'll al - ways sound pre - co - cious,

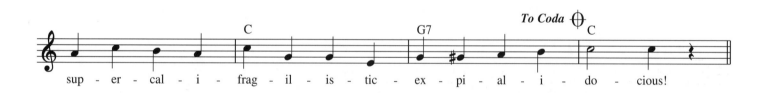

sup - er - cal - i - frag - il - is - tic - ex - pi - al - i - do - cious!

Bridge

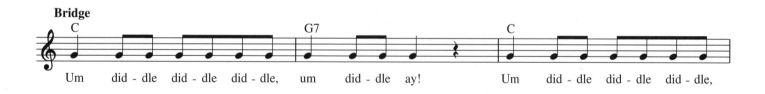

Um did - dle did - dle did - dle, um did - dle ay! Um did - dle did - dle did - dle,

Verse

um did - dle ay! Be - cause I was a - fraid to speak when

I was just a lad, me fa - ther gave me nose a tweak and

told me I was bad.   But then one day I learned a word that

saved me ach - in' nose,   the big - gest word you ev - er 'eard and

 *D.C. al Coda*    ⊕ *Coda*

this is 'ow it goes!   Oh!   do - cious!

Two Worlds
from Walt Disney Pictures' TARZAN™
Words and Music by Phil Collins

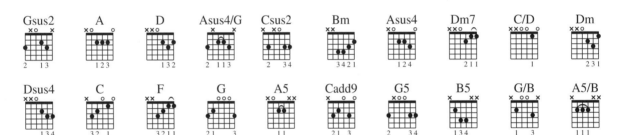

Strum Pattern: 2
Pick Pattern: 4

Chorus

Moderately

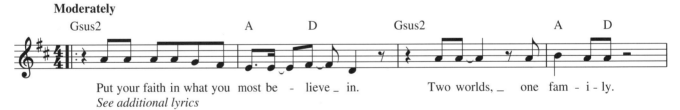

Put your faith in what you most be - lieve _ in.   Two worlds, _ one fam - i - ly.
See additional lyrics

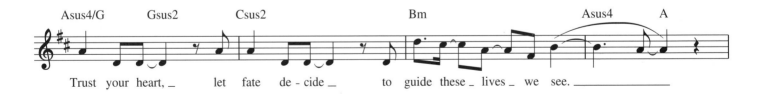

Trust your heart, _ let fate de - cide _ to guide these _ lives _ we see. _

A par - a - dise _ un - touched _ by man   with - in this _ world blessed with love.

Additional Lyrics

Chorus Softly tread the sand below your feet now.
Two worlds, one family.
Trust your heart, let the fate decide
To guide these lives we see.
Beneath the shelter of the trees,
Only love can enter here.
A simple life they live in peace.

These Are the Best Times

from Walt Disney Productions' SUPERDAD

Words and Music by Shane Tatum

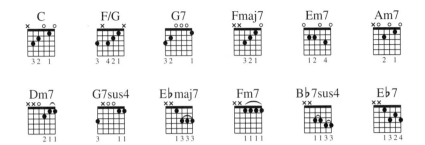

Strum Pattern: 1
Pick Pattern: 2

Verse

Moderately slow

1. These _ are the best times, _ the mo-ments we can't let slip _ a - way.
2. But once in a life - time, _ a min-ute like this is ours _ to share. Re-

1.

Life's lit - tle game _ we play, liv - ing from day to day. _____
mem - ber the mo - ments well, for

2.

Bridge

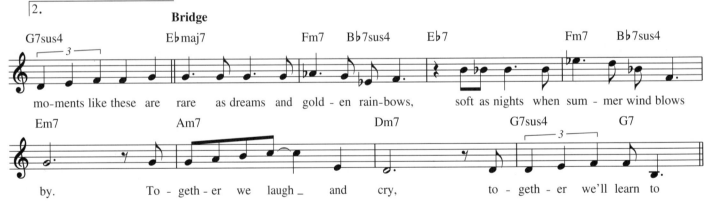

mo - ments like these are rare as dreams and gold - en rain - bows, soft as nights when sum - mer wind blows

by. To - geth - er we laugh _ and cry, to - geth - er we'll learn to

Outro-Verse

fly. Come take my hand, _____ to - geth - er we'll cross the time - less sands,

chas - ing the end - less sun, liv - ing our lives as one. _____

True to Your Heart

from Walt Disney Pictures' MULAN

Music by Matthew Wilder
Lyrics by David Zippel

Strum Pattern: 2
Pick Pattern: 4

Verse
Brightly

A7

1. Ba - by, I knew at once _ that you were meant for me. _ Deep _

_ in my soul, I know _ that I'm your des - ti - ny. _ Though you're un - sure, _ why

fight the tide? _ Don't think so much, _ let your heart de - cide. _ 2. Ba -

Verse

A7

- by, I see your fu - ture, and it's tied to mine. _ I look _ in your eyes and see _ you search - ing
3. *See additional lyrics*

for a sign. _ But you'll nev - er fall _ till you let go. _ Don't be so scared _ of what

Chorus

you don't _ know. True _ to your heart, you must _ be true _ to your heart. That's when _ the heav -

- ens will part, and ba - by, show - er you with my love. O - pen your eyes, your heart _ can tell _

Additional Lyrics

3. Someone ya know is on your side, can set you free.
I can do that for you if you believe in me.
Why second guess what feels so right?
Just trust your heart and you'll see the light.

Trust in Me
(The Python's Song)
from Walt Disney's THE JUNGLE BOOK

Words and Music by Richard M. Sherman and Robert B. Sherman

Strum Pattern: 3
Pick Pattern: 3

Verse
Moderately

The Unbirthday Song

from Walt Disney's ALICE IN WONDERLAND

Words and Music by Mack David, Al Hoffman and Jerry Livingston

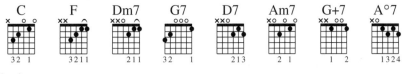

Strum Pattern: 3, 4
Pick Pattern: 1, 3

Under the Sea

from Walt Disney's THE LITTLE MERMAID

Lyrics by Howard Ashman
Music by Alan Menken

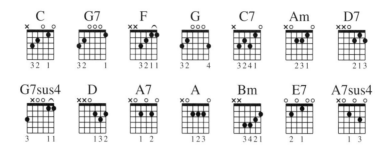

Strum Pattern: 4
Pick Pattern: 3

Additional Lyrics

2. Down here all the fish is happy
   As off through the wave they roll.
   The fish on the land ain't happy.
   They sad 'cause they in the bowl.
   But fish in the bowl is lucky,
   They in for a worser fate.
   One day when the boss get hungry
   Guess who gon' be on the plate.

Chorus Under the sea, under the sea.
   Nobody beat us, fry us and eat us in fricassee.
   We what the land folks loves to cook.
   Under the sea we off the hook.
   We got no troubles life is bubbles
   Under the sea.

Winnie the Pooh

from Walt Disney's THE MANY ADVENTURES OF WINNIE THE POOH

Words and Music by by Richard M. Sherman and Robert B. Sherman

A Whole New World

from Walt Disney's ALADDIN

Music by Alan Menken
Lyrics by Tim Rice

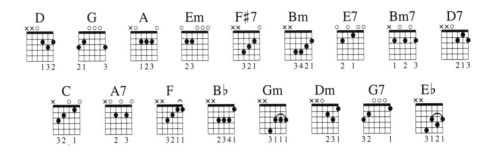

Strum Pattern: 4
Pick Pattern: 1

Verse
Moderately

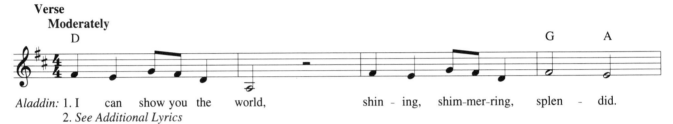

Aladdin: 1. I can show you the world, shin - ing, shim-mer-ring, splen - did.
2. *See Additional Lyrics*

Tell me prin-cess, now when did you last let your heart de - cide? ride. A whole new

Chorus

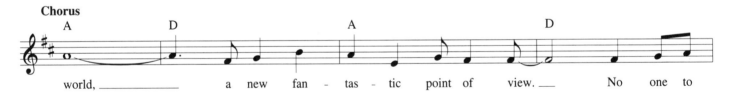

world, _____ a new fan - tas - tic point of view. __ No one to

tell us no, or where to go, or say we're on - ly dream - ing. *Jasmine:* A whole new

world, _____ a daz - zling place I nev - er knew. __ But, when I'm way up here, it's

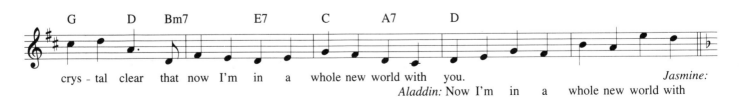

crys - tal clear that now I'm in a whole new world with you. *Jasmine:*
Aladdin: Now I'm in a whole new world with

Additional Lyrics

2. I can open your eyes,
   Take you wonder by wonder.
   Over, sideways and under
   On a magic carpet ride.

The Wonderful Thing About Tiggers

from Walt Disney's THE MANY ADVENTURES OF WINNIE THE POOH

Words and Music by Richard M. Sherman and Robert B. Sherman

Strum Pattern: 8
Pick Pattern: 8

Additional Lyrics

2. Oh, the wonderful thing about Tiggers
   Is Tiggers are wonderful chaps!
   They're loaded with vim and with vigor;
   They love to leap in your laps!
   They're jumpy, bumpy, clumpy, thumpy, fun, fun, fun, fun, fun!
   But the most wonderful thing about Tiggers is I'm the only one!

Woody's Roundup

from Walt Disney Pictures' TOY STORY 2 - A Pixar Film

Music and Lyrics by Randy Newman

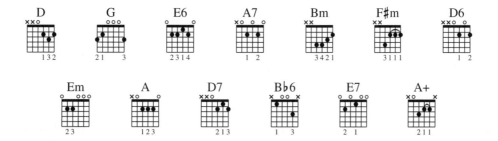

Strum Pattern: 10
Pick Pattern: 10

Verse

Brightly

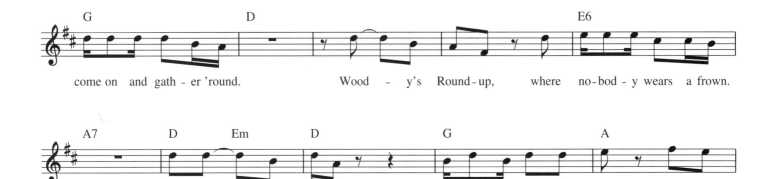

come on and gath-er 'round. Wood-y's Round-up, where no-bod-y wears a frown.

Bad guys __ go run-nin' when-ev-er he's in town. He's the

root-in'-est toot-in'-est shoot-in'-est hoot-in'-est cow-boy a-round. Wood-y's Round-up.

You've Got a Friend in Me

from Walt Disney's TOY STORY
from Walt Disney Pictures' TOY STORY 2 - A Pixar Film

Music and Lyrics by Randy Newman

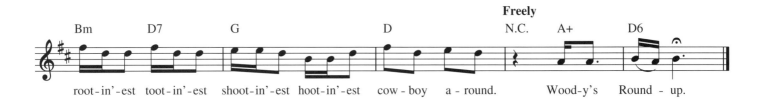

Strum Pattern: 2
Pick Pattern: 4

Verse

Easy shuffle

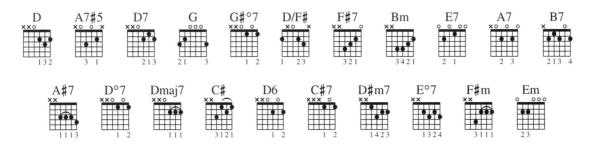

1. You've got a friend in me. __ You've got a friend in me.
2. *See additional lyrics*

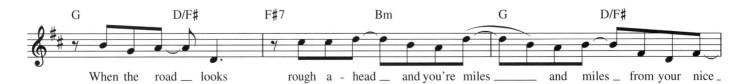

When the road __ looks rough a-head __ and you're miles __ and miles _ from your nice _

__ warm bed, __ you just re-mem-ber what your old pal said. __ Son, you've

Additional Lyrics

2. You've got a friend in me.
You've got a friend in me.
You got troubles, then I got 'em too.
There isn't anything I wouldn't do for you.
If we stick together we can see it through.
'Cause you've got a friend in me.
Yeah, you've got a friend in me.

The Work Song

from Walt Disney's CINDERELLA

Words and Music by Mack David, Al Hoffman and Jerry Livingston

Strum Pattern: 3, 4
Pick Pattern: 2, 3

Brightly

Verse

1. Cin - der - (2., 3.) el - la, Cin - der - el - la, all I hear is Cin - der -

el - la, from the mo - ment that I get up, till shades of night are fall - ing. There

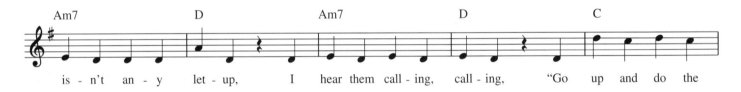

is - n't an - y let - up, I hear them call - ing, call - ing, "Go up and do the

To Coda

at - tic and go down and do the cel - lar, you can do them both to - geth - er, Cin - der -

Bridge

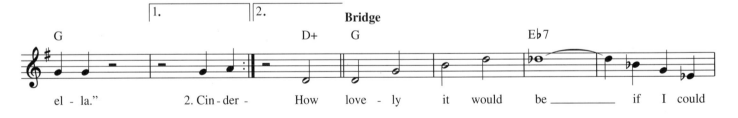

el - la." 2. Cin - der - How love - ly it would be _____ if I could

live my fan - ta - sy. _____ But in the mid - dle of my dream - ing _____

D.S. al Coda **Coda**

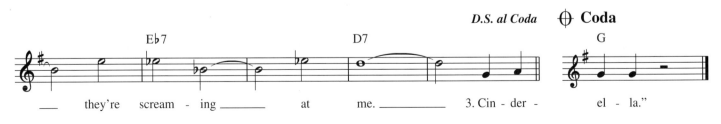

_____ they're scream - ing _____ at me. _____ 3. Cin - der - el - la."

Yo Ho
(A Pirate's Life for Me)

from Disneyland and Walt Disney World's PIRATES OF THE CARIBBEAN

Words by Xavier Atencio
Music by George Bruns

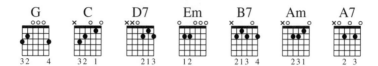

Strum Pattern: 8
Pick Pattern: 8

Verse
Moderately

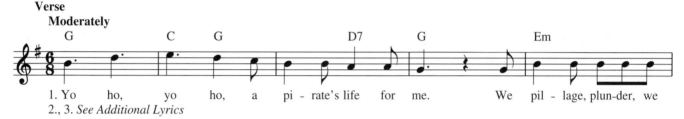

1. Yo ho, yo ho, a pi-rate's life for me. We pil-lage, plun-der, we
2., 3. *See Additional Lyrics*

ri-fle and loot. Drink up me 'eart-ies, yo ho. We kid-nap and rav-age and

don't give a hoot. Drink up me 'eart-ies, yo ho. up me 'eart-ies, yo

Outro

ho. We're ras-cals and scoun-drels, we're vil-lains and knaves. Drink up me 'eart-ies, yo

ho. We're dev-ils and black sheep, we're real-ly bad eggs. Drink up me 'eart-ies, yo

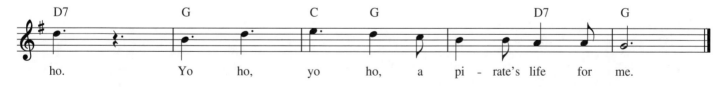

ho. Yo ho, yo ho, a pi-rate's life for me.

Additional Lyrics

2. Yo ho, yo ho, a pirate's life for me.
   We extort and pilfer, we filch and sack.
   Drink up me 'earties, yo ho.
   Maraud and embezzle and even highjack.
   Drink up me 'earties, yo ho.

3. Yo ho, yo ho, a pirate's life for me.
   We kindle and char and inflame and ignite.
   Drink up me 'earties, yo ho.
   We burn up the city, we're really a fright.
   Drink up me 'earties, yo ho.

You Can Fly! You Can Fly! You Can Fly!

from Walt Disney's PETER PAN

Words by Sammy Cahn
Music by Sammy Fain

Strum Pattern: 2, 3
Pick Pattern: 3, 4

Verse
Lively

1. Think of the pres-ents you're brought, an-y mer-ry lit-tle thought.
2., 3. *See Additional Lyrics*

Think of Christ-mas, think of snow, think of sleigh bells, here we go! Like rein-deer in the

sky _____ you can fly! You can fly! You can

fly! _____ fly! You can fly! You can fly! _____

Bridge

Soon you'll zoom all a-round the room, all it takes is faith and trust; but the thing that's a pos-i-tive

must is a lit-tle bit of Pix-ie Dust. The dust is a pos-i-tive must.

Coda

fly! You can fly! You can fly! _____

Additional Lyrics

2. Think of the happiest things,
   That's the way to get your wings.
   Now you own a candy store.
   Look! You're rising off the floor.
   Don't wonder how or why.
   You can fly! You can fly! You can fly!

3. When there's a smile in your heart,
   There's no better time to start.
   It's a very simple plan,
   You can do what birdies can;
   At least it's worth a try.
   You can fly! You can fly! You can fly!

You'll Be in My Heart
(Pop Version)

from Walt Disney Pictures' TARZAN ™

Words and Music by Phil Collins

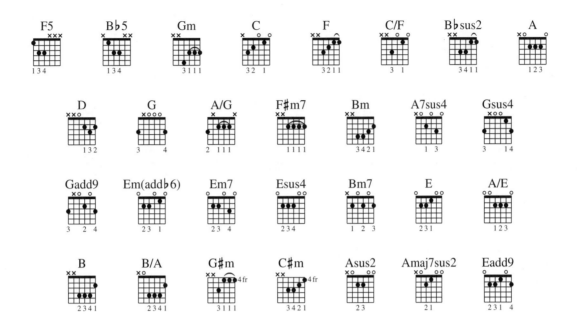

Strum Pattern: 2
Pick Pattern: 4

Intro

Moderately

Additional Lyrics

2. Why can't they understand the way we feel?
   They just don't trust what they can't explain.
   I know we're diff'rent, but deep inside us
   We're not that different at all.
   And you'll be in my heart,...

Bridge When destiny calls you
   You must be strong. (Gotta be strong.)
   It may not be with you,
   But you've got to hold on.
   They'll see in time, I know.

Zero to Hero

from Walt Disney Pictures' HERCULES

Music by Alan Menken
Lyrics by David Zippel

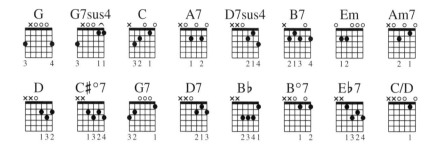

*Strum Pattern: 2
*Pick Pattern: 5

Verse
Moderately

1. Bless my soul, Herc _ was on a roll, per - son of the week in ev-'ry Greek o-pin-ion poll. _
3. *See additional lyrics*

*Use Pattern 10 for ²⁄₄ measures.

What a pro, Herc _ could stop a show. Point _ him at a mon-ster and you're talk-in' S. R. O. _

To Coda ⊕

He was a no __ one, a ze - ro, ze - ro. Now he's a hon - cho, he's a he - ro.

Verse

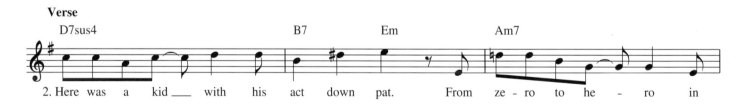

2. Here was a kid __ with his act down pat. From ze - ro to he - ro in

no __ time __ flat. __ Ze - ro to he - ro, just like that.

When he smiled _ the girls went wild with oohs __ and ahs. ___ And they

slapped his face __ on ev - 'ry vase. __ On ev - 'ry *vahse.* From ap -

pear-ance fees __ and roy - al - ties __ our Herc had cash to burn. _____ Now

nou - veau riche and fa - mous he could tell you what's a Gre - cian urn.

Coda   **Verse**

- ing bon - kers. __ 4. He showed the mox - ie, brains and spunk, from ze - ro to he - ro, a

ma - jor __ hunk. Ze - ro to he - ro *and who'd a thunk?*

Who put the glad in glad - i - a - tor?

Her - cu - les. Whose dar - ing deeds __ are great the - a - ter?

Her - cu - les. Is he bold? __ No one brav - er.

Is he sweet? __ Our fav - 'rite fla - vor. Her - cu - les.

Her - cu - les. Her - cu - les.

Outro

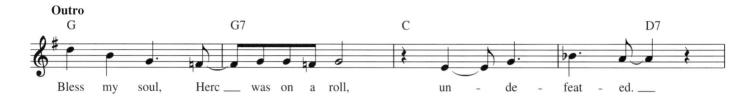

Bless my soul, Herc __ was on a roll, un - de - feat - ed. __

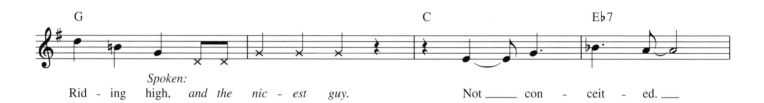

Spoken:
Rid - ing high, *and the nic - est guy.* Not __ con - ceit - ed. __

He was a noth - ing, ze - ro, ze - ro. Now he's a hon - cho, he's a he - ro.

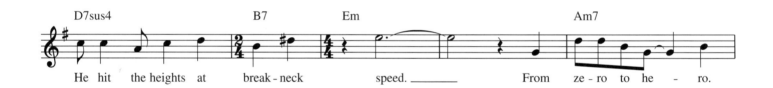

He hit the heights at break - neck speed. __ From ze - ro to he - ro.

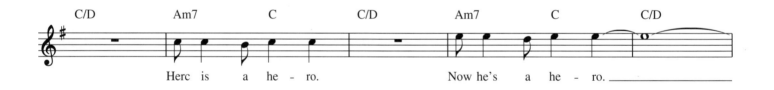

Herc is a he - ro. Now he's a he - ro. __

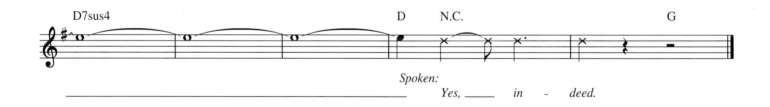

Spoken:
__ Yes, __ in - deed.

Additional Lyrics

3. Say amen there he goes again
   Sweet and undefeated and an awesome ten for ten
   Folks lined up just to watch him flex
   And this perfect package packed a pair of perfect pecs
   Hercie he comes he sees he conquers
   Honey the crowds were going bonkers

Zip-A-Dee-Doo-Dah

from Walt Disney's SONG OF THE SOUTH

Words by Ray Gilbert   Music by Allie Wrubel

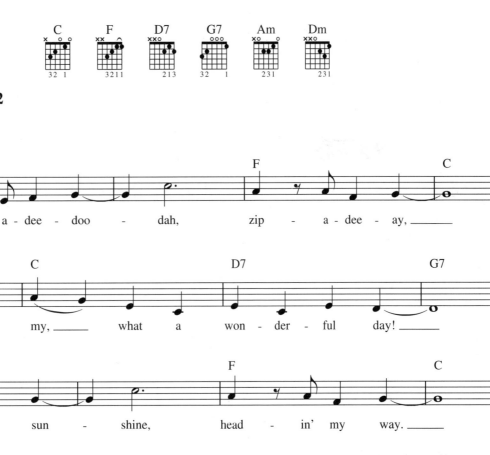

Strum Pattern: 2
Pick Pattern: 4

Chorus
Merrily

Zip - a - dee - doo - dah, zip - a - dee - ay, _____

My, oh my, _____ what a won - der - ful day! _____

Plen - ty of sun - shine, head - in' my way. _____

Zip - a - dee - doo - dah, zip - a - dee - ay! _____ Mis - ter

Verse

Blue - bird on my shoul - der. _____ It's the

truth, it's "act - ch'll". Ev - 'ry - thing is "sa - tis - fact - ch'll".

Outro-Chorus

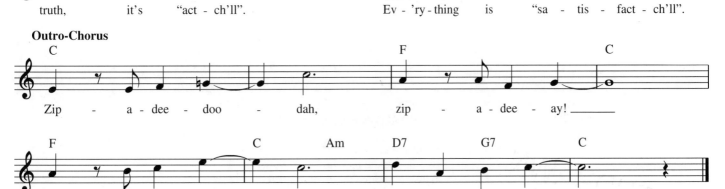

Zip - a - dee - doo - dah, zip - a - dee - ay!

Won - der - ful feel - ing, won - der - ful day. _____

Theme from Zorro

from the Television Series

Words by Norman Foster
Music by George Bruns

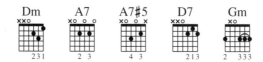

Strum Pattern: 7, 8
Pick Pattern: 8, 9

Additional Lyrics

2. He is polite,
   But the wicked take flight
   When they catch the sight of Zorro.
   He's friend of the weak
   And the poor and the meek,
   This very unique señor Zorro.